OCR GCSE Religious Studies A
World Religion(s)

Islam

Farzana Hassan · Russell Tomlinson · Cavan Wood

Series editor: Janet Dyson
Series consultant: Jon Mayled

www.heinemann.co.uk
✓ Free online support
✓ Useful weblinks
✓ 24 hour online ordering

01865 888080

OCR AND HEINEMANN ARE WORKING TOGETHER TO PROVIDE BETTER SUPPORT FOR YOU

Heinemann is an imprint of Pearson Education Limited, a company incorporated in England and Wales, having its registered office at Edinburgh Gate, Harlow, Essex, CM20 2JE. Registered company number: 872828

www.heinemann.co.uk

Heinemann is a registered trademark of Pearson Education Limited

Text © Pearson Education Limited 2009

First published 2009

13 12 11 10 09
10 9 8 7 6 5 4 3 2 1

British Library Cataloguing in Publication Data
A catalogue record for this book is available from the British Library.

ISBN 978-0-435-50134-1

Edited by Linda Free and Bruce Nicholson
Proofread by Tracey Smith
Reviewed by Imran Mogra (Birmingham City University)
Designed by Pearson Education Limited
Project managed and typeset by Wearset Ltd, Boldon, Tyne and Wear
Original illustrations © Pearson Education 2009
Illustrated by Wearset Ltd
Picture research by Q2AMedia
Cover photo/illustration © Frank van den Bergh/iStockPhoto
Printed by Rotolito, Italy

Acknowledgements
The author and publisher would like to thank the following individuals and organisations for permission to reproduce photographs:

Page 2 Frédéric Neema/Sygma/Corbis. Page 7 Christine Osborne/www.worldreligions.co.uk. Page 8 Berger Robert/Photolibrary. Page 10 Adam Woolfitt/Robert Harding. Page 12 Helene Rogers/Art Directors & Trip Photo Library. Page 15 Nazli. Page 16 Athar Akram/ArkReligion.com/Alamy. Page 18 Helene Rogers/Art Directors & Trip Photo Library. Page 20 Paul Thuysbaert/Photolibrary. Page 22 Ramzi Hachicho. Page 24 Mian Kursheed/Reuters. Page 25 Jane Mingay/Associated Press. Page 30t Aaron Favila/Associated Press. Page 30b Toby Melville/Reuters. Page 33r Ali Haider/EPA. Page 33m PhotoSky/Shutterstock. Page 34 Bk Bangash/Associated Press. Page 36 Romaanco Perfumers. Page 38 Frédéric Neema/Sygma/Corbis. Page 42 ayazad/Shutterstock. Page 43 Khayyam Wakil. Page 44 Muhannad Fala'ah/Stringer/Getty Images. Page 46 Christine Osborne/www.worldreligions.co.uk. Page 48 Douglas Miller/Stringer/Getty Images. Page 50 Helene Rogers/Art Directors & Trip Photo Library. Page 52 Shakil Adil/Associated Press. Page 58t Images & Stories/Alamy. Page 58b Stringer Pakistan/Reuters. Page 64 Gm1duvjnbhaa/Reuters. Page 67 Hadi Mizban/Associated Press. Page 68 Superstock/Photolibrary. Page 69 Ahmad Masood/Reuters. Page 70l Raheb Homavandi/Reuters. Page 70r John McConnico/Associated Press. Page 72 David Turnley/Corbis. Page 74 Ali Jasim/Reuters. Page 76 Assassin Films/The Kobal Collection/Buitendijk, Jaap. Page 77 Mai Chen/Alamy. Page 78 David Hoffman Photo Library/Alamy. Page 81 Ali Jarekji/Reuters. Page 86 Stuart Taylor/Shutterstock. Page 90 Stephen Trussler. Page 96 Walter Bibikow/JAI/Corbis. Page 98 Helene Rogers/Art Directors & Trip Photo Library. Page 100 Zainal Abd Halim/Reuters. Page 102 Andreu Dalmau/EFE/Corbis. Page 104 Sanjeev Gupta/EPA. Page 106 Janine Wiedel Photolibrary/Alamy. Page 108 Paul Sakuma/Associated Press. Page 114 Ahmad Faizal Yahya/Photographersdirect. Page 120 Helene Rogers/Alamy. Page 121 Bazuki Muhammad/Reuters. Page 122 Paul Gapper/World Religions Photo LIbrary. Page 124 Gary Roebuck/Alamy. Page 126 Earl & Nazima Kowall/Corbis. Page 127 Christine Osborne/Photographersdirect. Page 129 Steve Raymer/Jupiter Images. Page 130 Steve Raymer/Jupiter Images. Page 131 Dave Bartruff/Corbis. Page 134 Shirley Bahadur/Associated Press. Page 160 Valua Vitaly/Shutterstock. Page 146 Earl & Nazima Kowall/Corbis. Page 148 ArkReligion.com/Alamy. Page 150 Yamo/Dreamstime. Page 154 J A Giordano/Corbis Saba. Page 156 Helene Rogers/Art Directors & Trip Photo Library. Page 143 Aleksey Tkachenko/Istockphoto. Page 161 T.Mughal/EPA. Page 164 ArkReligion.com/Alamy.

Every effort has been made to contact copyright holders of material reproduced in this book. Any omissions will be rectified in subsequent printings if notice is given to the publishers.

Contents

Introduction

A note for teachers

This student book has been written especially to support the OCR Religious Studies Specification A, Units B577: *Islam 1* (Core beliefs, Special days and pilgrimage, Major divisions and interpretations) and B578: *Islam 2* (Places and forms of worship, Religion in the faith community and the family, Sacred writings). It is part of an overall series covering the OCR Specification A and comprising:

- a series of Student Books covering Christianity, Christianity from a Roman Catholic Perspective, Islam, Judaism and Perspectives on Christian Ethics – further details on pages viii and ix.
- a series of Teacher Guides: one covering Christianity, Islam and Judaism, and another three covering Buddhism, Hinduism and Sikhism – further details on pages viii and ix.

Who are we?

The people who have planned and contributed to this series of books include teachers, advisers, inspectors, teacher trainers and GCSE examiners, all of whom have specialist knowledge of Religious Studies. For all of us the subject has a real fascination and we believe that good Religious Studies can make a major contribution to developing the skills, insights and understanding people need in today's world. In the initial development of this series, Pamela Draycott lent us her expertise, which we gratefully acknowledge.

Why is Religious Studies an important subject?

We believe that Religious Studies is an important subject because every area of life is touched by issues to do with religion and belief. Following a Religious Studies GCSE course will enable students to study and explore what people believe about God, authority, worship, beliefs, values and truth. Students will have opportunities to engage with questions about why people believe in God and how beliefs can influence many aspects of their lives.

Students will also explore why members of a particular religion may believe different things. In lessons students will be expected to think, talk, discuss, question and challenge, reflect on and assess a wide range of

questions. As young people growing up in a diverse society studying religion will help them to understand and relate to people whose beliefs, values and viewpoints differ from their own, and help them to deal with issues arising, not only in school, but in the community and workplace.

The study of religion will also help students to make connections with a whole range of other important areas, such as music, literature, art, politics, economics and social issues.

The specification for OCR A Islam

The specification outlines the aims and purposes of GCSE and the content to be covered is divided into six different Topics. The book's structure follows these Topic divisions precisely:

Topic 1: Core beliefs

Topic 2: Special days and pilgrimage

Topic 3: Major divisions and interpretations

Topic 4: Places and forms of worship

Topic 5: Religion in the faith community and the family

Topic 6: Sacred writings

The Topics focus on developing skills such as analysis, empathy and evaluation, which will enable students to gain knowledge and understanding of the specified content.

In following this specification students will have the opportunity to study Islam in depth and will learn about diversity and the way in which people who believe in the religion follow its teachings in their everyday lives.

This book covers everything students will need to know for the examination and shows them how to use their knowledge and understanding to answer the questions they will be asked.

Changes to the specification

The specification has changed dramatically according to the developing nature of education and the need to meet the demands of the world for students. The new specification will be taught from September 2009 onwards. The main changes that teachers and students should be aware of include the following:

- The Assessment Objectives (AOs) have changed, with a 50% focus now given to AO1 (Describe, explain and analyse, using knowledge and understanding) and a 50% focus to AO2 (Use evidence and reasoned argument to express and evaluate personal responses, informed insights and differing viewpoints). Previously, the balance was 75% to 25% respectively. There is more information on this on pages x and xi.

- There is an increased focus on learning *from* religion rather than simply learning *about* religion, and explicit reference to religious beliefs is now required in answers marked by Levels of Response.

- Levels of Response grids have been changed to a new range of 0–6 marks for AO1 questions and 0–12 marks for AO2 questions. See pages x and xi for the complete grids.

- Quality of Written Communication (QWC) is now only assessed on parts (d) and (e) of each question.

- Beyond the six Islam Topics covered by this book, there is now a greater choice of Topics within the specification including a new Christian Scriptures paper on the Gospels of Mark and Luke, a paper on Muslim texts and a paper on Jewish texts.

- There is also more freedom to study different combinations of religions and Topics.

Why did we want to write these resources?

We feel strongly that there is a need for good classroom resources, which take advantage of the changed Assessment Objectives, and which:

- make the subject lively, interactive and relevant to today's world

- encourage students to talk to each other and work together

- challenge students and encourage them to think in depth in order to reach a high level of critical thinking

- train students to organise their thoughts in writing in a persuasive and structured way, and so prepare them for examination.

The book has many features which contribute towards these goals. **Grade Studio** provides stimulating and realistic exercises to train students in what examiners are looking for and how to meet those expectations. **Exam Café** provides an exciting environment in which students can plan and carry out their revision.

Of course learning is about more than just exams. Throughout the book you will find **Research Notes**, which encourage students to explore beyond the book and beyond the curriculum. All of these features are explained in more detail on the next two pages.

What is in this book?

This student book has the following sections;

- the **Introduction**, which you are reading now
- the six **Topics** covered in the specification
- **Exam Café** – an invaluable resource for students studying their GCSE in Religious Studies
- **Glossary** – a reference tool for key terms and words used throughout the book.

Each of the above is covered in more detail in the text below.

The six Topics

Each Topic in this book contains:

- a Topic scene-setter (**The Big Picture**)
- a look at the key questions raised by the Topic, and the key words and issues associated with those questions (**Develop your knowledge**)
- two-page spreads covering the **main Topic content**
- two pages of different level questions to check understanding of the Topic material (**Remember and Reflect**)
- exam-style questions with level indicators, examiner's comments and model answers (**Grade Studio**).

These features, which are explained more fully in the following pages, have been carefully planned and designed to draw together the OCR specification in an exciting but manageable way.

The Big Picture

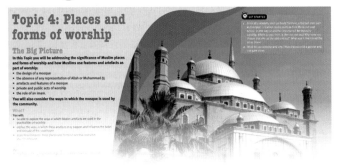

This provides an overview of the Topic. It explains to students **what** they will be studying (the content), **how** they will study it (the approaches, activities and tasks) and

why they are studying it (the rationale). It also includes a **Get started** activity, often linked to a picture or visual stimuli, which presents a task designed to engage students in the issues of the Topic and give them some idea of the content to be studied.

Develop your knowledge

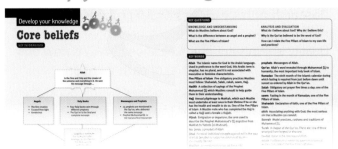

This lists the **key information**, **key questions** and **key words** of the Topic. At a glance, it allows students to grasp the basic elements of knowledge they will gain in the study of the Topic. It is also a useful reference point for reflection and checking information as it is studied.

Main Topic content

The main content of each Topic is covered in a number of two-page spreads. Each spread equates to roughly one lesson of work – although teachers will need to judge for themselves if some of these need more time.

Each spread begins with the learning outcomes, highlighted in a box at the top of the page, so that students are aware of the focus and aims of the lesson. The text then attempts to answer, through a balanced viewpoint, one or two of the key questions raised in

Develop your knowledge. The text carefully covers the views of both religious believers and non-believers. It is also punctuated with activities that range from simple tasks that can take place in the classroom to more complex tasks that can be tackled away from school.

A range of margin features adds extra depth and support to the main text both for students and the teacher.

- **For debate** invites students to examine two sides of a controversial issue.
- **Must think about!** directs students towards a key idea that they should consider.
- **Sacred text** provides an extract from one of the religions covered in the Topic to help students understand religious ideas and teachings.
- **Research notes** provide stimulating ideas for further research beyond the material covered in the book and in the OCR specification.

Activities

Every Topic has a range of interesting activities which will help students to achieve the learning outcomes. Every two-page spread has a short starter activity to grab students' attention and to get them thinking (see **Get Started** activity above). This is followed by a development section where the main content is introduced, and a plenary activity, which may ask students to reflect on what they have learnt, or may start them thinking about the next steps.

All activities are labelled AO1 or AO2 so you can tell at a glance which skills will be developed.

Remember and Reflect

This provides an opportunity for students to reflect on what they have learned and identify possible weaknesses or gaps in their knowledge. It also helps them to recognise key ideas in the specification content. Once they have tested their knowledge with the first set of questions, a cross-reference takes them back to the relevant part of the text so they can check their answers. A second set of questions helps them to develop the AO2 skills necessary for the examination.

What is Grade Studio?

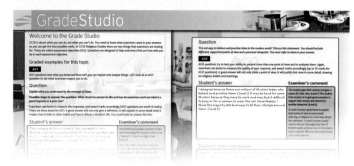

Everyone has different learning needs and this section of the book gives clear focus on how, with guidance from the teacher, students can develop the skills that will help them to achieve the higher levels in their exam responses.

Grade Studio appears as boxes within each Topic, as well as a two-page spread at the end of every Topic. It includes tips from the examiner, guidance on the steps to completing a well structured answer, and sample answers with examiner comments.

What is the Exam Café?

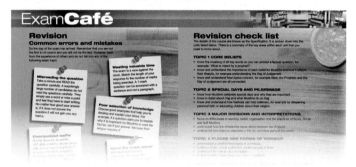

This is the revision section of the book. Here students will find useful revision tools and tips on how to get started on their revision and exam preparation. Students will also find assessment advice, including examples of different types of questions and samples of frequently asked questions. A useful **revision check list** allows students to review each Topic's content and explains where to find material in the book that relates to the exam questions.

Exam Café also has:

- sample student answers with examiner's comments
- help on understanding exam language, so students can achieve higher grades
- examiner tips, including common mistakes to be avoided.

Heinemann's OCR Religious Studies A Series

Below is a snapshot of the complete OCR Religious Studies A series. Further detail can be found at www.heinemann.co.uk/gcse.

OCR A Teacher Guide – Christianity, Islam and Judaism

ISBN 978-0-435-50136-5

This Teacher Guide covers Christianity, Islam and Judaism. It corresponds throughout to the Student Books and contains lesson plans, worksheets and Grade Studios to provide a complete teaching course for the chosen religion(s). The Christianity section of the Teacher Guide covers each Topic in the specification with six sample lesson plans and worksheets. The other religions have three sample lesson plans and worksheets. Everything is cross referenced to the student books to help you make the most out of these resources.

The Teacher Guide comes with a Resource Browser CD-ROM, which contains all the lesson plans along with a fully customisable version of all the worksheets.

Perspectives on Christian Ethics Student Book

ISBN 978-0-435-50270-6

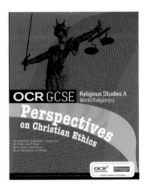

This book provides complete coverage of both units of Christian Ethics (B589 and B603). It provides information, activities, and Grade Studio examples for all aspects of the course, as well as an 8-page Exam Café for revision. Teachers will find support for almost all aspects of this course in the OCR B Teacher Guide: Philosophy and Applied Ethics (ISBN 978-0-435-50152-5).

Christianity Student Book

ISBN 978-0-435-50130-3

This book provides complete coverage of both units of Christianity (B571 and B572). It provides information, activities, and Grade Studio examples for all aspects of the course, as well as an 8-page Exam Café for revision. Comprehensive support for the Teacher is provided through the corresponding OCR A Teacher Guide (see above).

Judaism Student Book

ISBN 978-0-435-50133-4

This book provides complete coverage of both units of Judaism (B579 and B580). It provides information, activities, and Grade Studio examples for all aspects of the course, as well as an 8-page Exam Café for revision. Comprehensive support for the Teacher is provided through the corresponding OCR A Teacher Guide (see above).

Roman Catholic Student Book

ISBN 978-0-435-50132-7

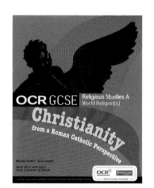

This book provides complete coverage of both units of Christianity (Roman Catholic) (B573 and B574). It provides information, activities, and Grade Studio examples for all aspects of the course, as well as an 8-page Exam Café for revision.

OCR A Teacher Guide – Buddhism

ISBN 978-0-435-50129-7

This Teacher Guide covers Buddhism. It contains lesson plans, worksheets and Grade Studios to provide a complete teaching course for Buddhism. It covers Units B569 and B570 in the OCR A specification.

OCR A Teacher Guide – Hinduism

ISBN 978-0-435-50128-0

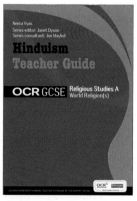

This Teacher Guide covers Hinduism. It contains lesson plans, worksheets and Grade Studios to provide a complete teaching course for Hinduism. It covers Units B575 and B576 in the OCR A specification.

OCR A Teacher Guide – Sikhism

ISBN 978-0-435-50127-3

This Teacher Guide covers Sikhism. It contains lesson plans, worksheets and Grade Studios to provide a complete teaching course for Sikhism. It covers Units B581 and B582 in the OCR A specification.

Assessment Objectives and Levels of Response

Assessment Objectives, AO1 and AO2

In the new specification, the questions in the examination are designed to test students against two Assessment Objectives: AO1 and AO2. In the specification 50% of the marks will be awarded for AO1 questions and 50% will be awarded for AO2 questions.

AO1 Questions require candidates to 'describe, explain and analyse, using knowledge and understanding'.

AO2 Questions require candidates to 'use evidence and reasoned argument to express and evaluate personal responses, informed insights, and differing viewpoints'.

Each question in the examination is composed of 5 parts, a–e. In more detail:

- Parts **a–c** are worth one, two and three marks respectively and test a candidate's knowledge (AO1 skills).
- Part **d** is worth six marks and tests a candidate's understanding (AO1 skills).
- Part **e** is worth twelve marks and tests a candidate's AO2 skills.

LEVELS OF RESPONSE FOR MARKING AO1 PART (D) QUESTIONS

LEVEL 1

(1–2 marks)

A **weak** attempt to answer the question.

Candidates will demonstrate little understanding of the question.
- A small amount of relevant information may be included.
- Answers may be in the form of a list with little or no description/explanation/analysis.
- There will be little or no use of specialist terms.
- Answers may be ambiguous or disorganised.
- Errors of grammar, punctuation and spelling may be intrusive.

LEVEL 2

(3–4 marks)

A **satisfactory** answer to the question.

Candidates will demonstrate some understanding of the question.
- Information will be relevant but may lack specific detail.
- There will be some description/explanation/analysis although this may not be fully developed.
- The information will be presented for the most part in a structured format.
- Some use of specialist terms, although these may not always be used appropriately.
- There may be errors in spelling, grammar and punctuation.

LEVEL 3

(5–6 marks)

A **good** answer to the question.

Candidates will demonstrate a clear understanding of the question.
- A fairly complete and full description/explanation/analysis.
- A comprehensive account of the range and depth of relevant material.
- The information will be presented in a structured format.
- There will be significant, appropriate and correct use of specialist terms.
- There will be few, if any, errors in spelling, grammar and punctuation.

LEVELS OF RESPONSE FOR MARKING AO2 PART (E) QUESTIONS

LEVEL 0

(0 marks)

No evidence submitted or response does not address the question.

LEVEL 1

(1–3 marks)

A **weak** attempt to answer the question.

Candidates will demonstrate little understanding of the question.

- Answers may be simplistic with little or no relevant information.
- Viewpoints may not be supported or appropriate.
- Answers may be ambiguous or disorganised.
- There will be little or no use of specialist terms.
- Errors of grammar, punctuation and spelling may be intrusive.

LEVEL 2

(4–6 marks)

A **limited** answer to the question.

Candidates will demonstrate some understanding of the question.

- Some information will be relevant, although may lack specific detail.
- Only one view might be offered and developed.
- Viewpoints might be stated and supported with limited argument/discussion.
- The information will show some organisation.
- Reference to the religion studied may be vague.
- Some use of specialist terms, although these may not always be used appropriately.
- There may be errors in spelling, grammar and punctuation.

LEVEL 3

(7–9 marks)

A **competent** answer to the question.

Candidates will demonstrate a sound understanding of the question.

- Selection of relevant material with appropriate development.
- Evidence of appropriate personal response.
- Justified arguments/different points of view supported by some discussion.
- The information will be presented in a structured format.
- Some appropriate reference to the religion studied.
- Specialist terms will be used appropriately and for the most part correctly.
- There may be occasional errors in spelling, grammar and punctuation.

LEVEL 4

(10–12 marks)

A **good** answer to the question.

Candidates will demonstrate a clear understanding of the question.

- Answers will reflect the significance of the issue(s) raised.
- Clear evidence of an appropriate personal response, fully supported.
- A range of points of view supported by justified arguments/discussion.
- The information will be presented in a clear and organised way.
- Clear reference to the religion studied.
- Specialist terms will be used appropriately and correctly.
- Few, if any, errors in spelling, grammar and punctuation.

Topic 1: Core beliefs

The Big Picture

In this Topic you will be addressing Islamic beliefs and practices about:

- the nature of Allah
- the Day of Judgement and life after death
- the life and teaching of Muhammad ﷺ
- the practice of the Five Pillars of Islam
- greater and lesser jihad.

You will also consider the ways in which these beliefs affect the lifestyles and outlook of Muslims in the modern world.

What?

You will:

- develop your knowledge and understanding of core Muslim beliefs
- explain what these beliefs mean to Muslims and think about how they might affect how Muslims live
- make links between these beliefs and what you think or believe.

How?

By:

- recalling and selecting information about the core Muslim beliefs and explaining their importance to Muslims today
- thinking about the relevance of Muslim belief in the 21st century
- evaluating your own views about these Muslim beliefs.

Why?

Because:

- these core beliefs underpin, and are reflected in, Muslim practices (such as the practice of the Five Pillars)
- understanding Muslim beliefs can help you understand why Muslims think and act in the way they do
- understanding these beliefs helps you to compare and contrast what others believe, including thinking about your own ideas and beliefs.

A Muslim family in Cairo.

1 Which statement is the odd one out and why?
   a The chemical symbol for copper is Cu.
   b *Strictly Come Dancing* is the best television show in the world.
   c The circumference of the earth at the equator is 40,075 km.

2 What is the difference between fact, opinion and belief?

3 What is the difference between belief and faith?

Develop your knowledge

Core beliefs

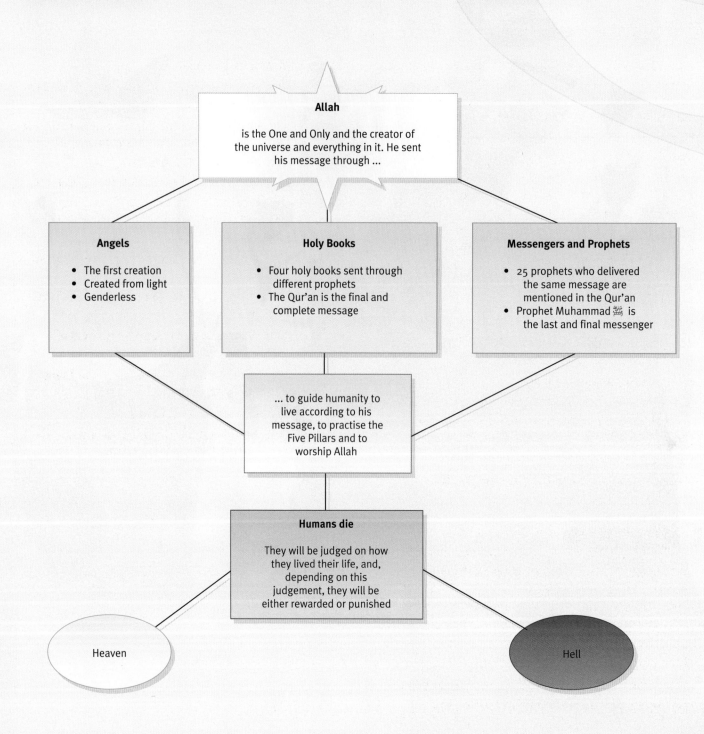

Allah

is the One and Only and the creator of the universe and everything in it. He sent his message through ...

Angels

- The first creation
- Created from light
- Genderless

Holy Books

- Four holy books sent through different prophets
- The Qur'an is the final and complete message

Messengers and Prophets

- 25 prophets who delivered the same message are mentioned in the Qur'an
- Prophet Muhammad ﷺ is the last and final messenger

... to guide humanity to live according to his message, to practise the Five Pillars and to worship Allah

Humans die

They will be judged on how they lived their life, and, depending on this judgement, they will be either rewarded or punished

Heaven

Hell

KNOWLEDGE AND UNDERSTANDING

What do Muslims believe about God?

What is the difference between an angel and a prophet?

What are the Five Pillars of Islam?

ANALYSIS AND EVALUATION

What do I believe about God? Why do I believe this?

Why is the Qur'an believed to be the word of God?

How can I relate the Five Pillars of Islam to my own life and practices?

KEY WORDS

Allah The Islamic name for God in the Arabic language. Used in preference to the word God, this Arabic term is singular, has no plural, and it is not associated with masculine or feminine characteristics.

Five Pillars of Islam Five obligatory practices Muslims must follow: Shahadah, Salah, zakah, sawm, Hajj.

Hadith A collection of sayings of the Prophet Muhammad ﷺ which Muslims consult to help guide them in their understanding.

Hajj Annual pilgrimage to Makkah, which each Muslim must undertake at least once in their lifetime if he or she has the health and wealth to do so. One of the Five Pillars of Islam. A Muslim male who has completed the Hajj is called a Hajji and a female a Hajjah.

Hijrah Emigration or departure; the term used to describe the Prophet Muhammad's ﷺ migration from Makkah to Yathrib (al-Madinah).

Isa Jesus; a prophet of Allah.

jihad Personal individual struggle against evil in the way of Allah (greater) or collective defence of the Muslim community (lesser).

khalifah Steward or custodian (of the earth).

Muhammad ﷺ The name of the final prophet.

prophets Messengers of Allah.

Qur'an Allah's word revealed through Muhammad ﷺ to humanity; the most important holy book of Islam.

Ramadan The ninth month of the Islamic calendar during which fasting is required from just before dawn until sunset as ordered by Allah in the Qur'an.

Salah Obligatory set prayer five times a day; one of the Five Pillars of Islam.

sawm Fasting in the month of Ramadan; one of the Five Pillars of Islam.

Shahadah Declaration of faith; one of the Five Pillars of Islam.

shirk Associating anything with God; the most serious sin that a Muslim can commit.

Sunnah Model practices, customs and traditions of Muhammad ﷺ.

Surah A chapter of the Qur'an. There are 114 of these arranged from longest to shortest.

tawhid Belief in the Oneness of Allah.

zakah Purification of wealth by payment of annual welfare due; one of the Five Pillars of Islam.

FOR INTEREST

Historically, Muhammad ﷺ had been slandered and persecuted, and he even had to leave his home town of Makkah when his life and the lives of his companions were threatened. He migrated to al-Madinah where he was allowed to spread the word of Allah. Muhammad ﷺ became a great leader and is the great model for Muslims today.

Have you ever had to stop or leave something that was special or meant something important to you?

Do Muslims believe in One God?

Islam

Islam is an Arabic word meaning 'peace' and 'submission to **Allah**'. This is because if people believe in Allah and the Oneness of Allah then they should submit only to Allah and follow what Allah has ordained. Therefore a Muslim is someone who chooses to submit to Allah.

Allah

Allah means 'Supreme Essence' which indicates all of Allah's attributes.

- Allah is the Muslim name for God.
- Allah is a specific name used only for God and is never used for any other being.
- The name Allah cannot be plural in Arabic and therefore cannot be used to refer to more than one.
- The Ninety-Nine Names of God: 'To Him belong the Most Beautiful Names' (from **Surah** 59:24). (A Surah is a chapter of the **Qur'an**.)
- The Ninety-Nine Names are qualities or attributes of God but they do not describe God's essence which is only done through the name Allah.
- The nature of God is summed up in these Ninety-Nine Names.
- All of these names are found in the Qur'an.
- Muslims are encouraged to learn, recite and live by these Ninety-Nine Names by embracing the qualities described in the names (for example, to be kind, generous, compassionate and giving).

Tawhid

Tawhid is an Arabic word that means 'belief in the Oneness of Allah'. This concept derives from the Qur'an itself which describes the nature of God as One, who is Unique, Everlasting, Eternal, Absolute, and there is none like him. This means God has always been in existence and always will be in existence.

> **Surah 112:1–4**
> *Say: He is Allah, the One and Only;*
> *Allah, the Eternal, Absolute;*
> *He begetteth not, nor is He begotten;*
> *And there is none like unto Him.*

God's nature

- It is important for Muslims to understand the nature of God's mercy and compassion so that they can seek forgiveness for their shortcomings.
- The Qur'an is a great example of God's mercy and compassion as every Surah of the Qur'an (except Surah 9) begins with a reference to mercy and compassion.
- Muslims believe that humans are **khalifahs** (stewards) on earth and that they should take care of it as God has guided them to do.
- Allah did not simply create humans and then leave them to it; Allah through mercy and compassion sent them **prophets**, and Allah's word shows them and guides them how to live.

Tawhid and creation

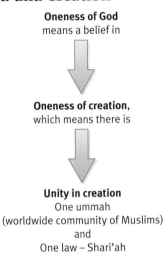

Oneness of God
means a belief in

Oneness of creation,
which means there is

Unity in creation
One ummah
(worldwide community of Muslims)
and
One law – Shari'ah

The Adhan is whispered into a baby's ear.

Tawhid in Muslim life

It is important for Muslims to declare that there is only One God – Allah – and to believe this. If they believe in tawhid – the Oneness of God – then they need to adhere to this and live their life according to it.

This is accomplished by ensuring that they do not commit **shirk** (associating anything with God). This is the most serious sin that a Muslim can commit. Associating something with God can also mean worshipping or following something other than God, such as the love of money.

- In order to help Muslims avoid idol worship or refer to a picture as God, Muslims do not have any pictures or statues in mosques. The only artworks found in mosques are calligraphy and geometric patterns (see page 93).
- The Oneness of God should be the first thing a baby hears. The father whispers the **Adhan** (call to prayer) in the baby's right ear and then the Iqamah, the command to rise and worship, into the left ear. This is to ensure that the baby grows up obedient and is set on the right path from the moment of birth.
- The **Shahadah** (declaration of faith) should be the last words uttered or heard by a dying Muslim. If the dying person is not able to say the Shahadah then it is said by the other people who are there. This is because life begins and is sealed with the ending of the Shahadah – the statement of belief in Allah and Allah's greatness and that **Muhammad** ﷺ is Allah's messenger.

AO2
skills **ACTIVITIES**

'It is too hard for a Muslim to avoid shirk because everyone follows pop groups or footballers.' Do you agree? Give reasons to support your opinion and also say how a Muslim might respond to this statement.

What is the message that Muslims must believe in?

The next two pages will help you to:

- identify how the message was delivered
- examine the three different channels through which the message was sent – angels, holy books, prophets
- evaluate the importance of these in relation to Muslim belief.

 **ACTIVITIES**

Make a list explaining what Muslims believe about angels. Now compare this to a list of what you have learnt elsewhere about angels. What are the differences and similarities?

 **RESEARCH NOTE**

Find out more about the different holy books. What are the differences between them?

Even when old, copies of the Qur'an are treated with great respect.

The message of Islam

The message of Islam was delivered through:

- angels
- holy books
- messengers and prophets.

 **ACTIVITIES**

Research a list of the prophets mentioned in the Qur'an. Identify if any of these prophets are also linked with Judaism and Christianity.

Angels

- Angels are immortal.
- Unlike humans, angels do not have free will and therefore can do nothing against the will of God.
- Angels are without sin.
- Islam teaches that angels are made of light and are genderless.

Nature of angels

Angels are described as having wings but Muslims cannot imagine any more about their appearance: 'who made the angels, messengers with wings – two, or three, or four (pairs)' (from **Surah** 35:1).

The angels praise God in heaven and they are guardians of hell. They have different roles and responsibilities and evidence of this is found in the **Qur'an**: 'We have set none but angels as guardians of the fire' (from Surah 74:31).

Functions of angels

- Muslims do not know how many angels there are. There are many angels which fill the whole of creation. They are a way in which **Allah** communicates with humans and they also perform tasks such as those listed below. Although Muslims do not know exactly how many angels there are, they refer to the ten main angels which are mentioned in the Qur'an. These are:
  - Jibril (Gabriel) in charge of wahi (revelation);
  - Mika'il in charge of heavenly affairs;
  - Israfil in charge of blowing the trumpet;
  - Asra'il Angel of death;
  - Rakeeb and Atheed, noble writers, in charge of recording deeds;
  - Munkar and Nakir in charge of questioning in the grave;
  - Ridwan in charge of heaven (gatekeeper);
  - Maalik in charge of hell (gatekeeper).

Holy books

The Qur'an is the literal word of God revealed to the Prophet **Muhammad** ﷺ through the angel Jibril. It is the holy book for all Muslims to follow until the end of time.

There are other holy books which are a part of Muslim belief and which all Muslims must believe God sent to humanity:

- Sahifah – the scroll revealed to the prophet Ibrahim (Abraham)
- Tawrah – the book given to the prophet Musa (Moses)
- Zabur – the Book of Psalms given to the prophet Dawud (David)
- Injil (Gospels) – the book given to the prophet **Isa** (Jesus).

The Qur'an

The Qur'an is the basis of Shari'ah, the set of laws to which Muslims must adhere. Muslims believe that:

- the Qur'an is the literal word of God, which God revealed to the Prophet Muhammad ﷺ through the angel Jibril;
- the Qur'an was memorised by Muhammad ﷺ, who then dictated it to his companions. They too memorised it, wrote it down, and reviewed it with the Prophet Muhammad ﷺ;
- not one letter of the Qur'an has been changed over the centuries since its revelation;
- the Qur'an, which was revealed fourteen centuries ago, mentioned facts only recently discovered or proven by scientists.

Muslims are encouraged to study the Qur'an and some even memorise it letter by letter: 'If ye do believe in Allah and in the revelation We sent down to Our servant on the Day of Testing – the Day of the meeting of the two forces. For Allah hath power over all things' (from Surah 8:41).

Prophets

- Some people say that there have been 124,000 **prophets**.
- The prophets were sent to teach God's word and to guide humanity: 'To every people (was sent) an apostle' (from Surah 10:47).
- These messengers are not angels, they are humans: 'Ye are no more than human, like ourselves!' (from Surah 14:10).
- According to the Qur'an, each prophet was given God's word for their generation. However, their words were distorted and changed by the people who heard them, so God had to send a new prophet with the original message.
- Muhammad ﷺ received the Qur'an from God. The Qur'an remains unchanged and the message is no longer distorted, so there have been no prophets since Muhammad ﷺ. Muhammad ﷺ is the last prophet.

Is there an afterlife?

Akhirah

Akhirah is an Arabic word meaning 'everlasting life after death'. Akhirah consists of:

- the last day
- the Day of Judgement
- heaven or hell.

Nature of humanity

Intellect is the human faculty which makes us different from animals. The fact that humans know that they will die is another difference between humans and animals.

God has given Muslims knowledge and guidance (the **Qur'an** and **Sunnah**) to show them how to live their life, but it is up to them to follow this advice. Muslims believe that humans are **khalifahs** (stewards) on earth and are thinking, rational creatures. They believe that this temporal life on earth is not all that there is. This earthly life is simply a preparation for the life to come. What happens to an individual in the afterlife depends on how they lived on earth.

Life is a test

- All Muslims must believe in akhirah, everlasting life after death.
- It is obvious to Muslims that eternal life is far more important than their life on earth, which is short compared with eternal life, and so a Muslim should work towards eternal life.
- Muslims believe that life on earth has a very important purpose – it is a test:

> ### Surah 2:155
> *Be sure we shall test you with something of fear and hunger, some loss in goods or lives or the fruits (of your toil), but give glad tidings to those who patiently persevere.*

- No matter what people have or do not have, it will be accounted for when they are judged. There is no point in asking 'Why am I not rich?' or 'Why am I not beautiful?' People cannot know these reasons or what God intends them to learn. To a Muslim it is all God's will:

> ### Hadith
> *When you see a person who has been given more than you in money and beauty, look to those, who have been given less.*

The next two pages will help you to:

- examine what Muslims believe about the afterlife
- evaluate the different stages of life after death and how these relate to a Muslim's life.

ACTIVITIES

What is your understanding of the 'last day'?

Graves in the cemetery of an old mosque in the Maldives.

What is tested?

- Character – whether someone is greedy, selfish, lacking in sympathy.
- Reaction to misfortune – whether someone is full of complaints, a burden to others, becomes depressed.
- Reaction to good fortune – whether someone is selfish, conceited, arrogant or becomes too proud.
- Way of life – whether someone is dishonest, disrespectful, hurtful or unforgiving.

The Book of Deeds

Muslims believe that all people earn, or are responsible for, their own salvation (whether they are judged fit for heaven or are sent to hell) as a result of their actions throughout their life. This means that they should not rely on anyone except themselves for salvation. It is important for them to acknowledge that all deeds, whether good or bad, affect only them and that all their actions have a direct effect on their salvation.

In Muslim belief there are two angels, Rakeeb and Atheed, who are the noble writers, whose role is to note down every deed. Therefore all of our actions, whether good or bad, are known and are recorded. This record is called the Book of Deeds, and it will be handed to the individual on the Day of Judgement:

> **Surah 41:46**
>
> *Whoever works righteousness benefits his own soul; whoever works evil, it is against his own soul: nor is thy Lord ever unjust (in the least) to His Servants.*

> **Surah 17:13–14**
>
> *Every man's fate We have fastened on his own neck: On the Day of Judgment We shall bring out for him a scroll, which he will see spread open. (It will be said to him:) 'Read thine (own) record: Sufficient is thy soul this day to make out an account against thee.'*

Stages of the afterlife

- Barzakh (barrier) – The state of waiting between the moment of death and the Day of Judgement.
- End of the world – This is vividly explained in the Qur'an:

> **Surah 39:68**
>
> *The Trumpet will (just) be sounded, when all that are in the heavens and on earth will swoon, except such as it will please **Allah** (to exempt). Then will a second one be sounded, when, behold, they will be standing and looking on!*

- Day of Judgement – Accountability for one's earthly life, as recorded in the Book of Deeds.
- Eternal afterlife – A different dimension to that of the earthly life; either heaven (paradise; the reward for a good life) or hell (punishment for a bad life).

FOR DEBATE

'Allah intends that everyone should share their wealth so not helping the poor is the same as stealing from them.'

AO1 skills **ACTIVITIES**

Match the terms in group A with their explanations in group B.

Group A: Qur'an; shirk; Muhammad ﷺ; Shahadah; akhirah; angels; Day of Judgement; death.

Group B: reward or punishment; end of the test; immortal and do nothing against the will of God; last of the prophets; declaration of faith; associating something with God; holy book; life after death.

Choose three terms from the following list and ensure they are linked, for example, *Allah* created the *Angels* then *humans*. For each chosen term, write a paragraph using information from this Topic:

Afterlife; heaven; evil deeds; Allah; akhirah; angels; Qur'an; death; Day of Judgement; hell; Muhammad ﷺ; Adam (Topic 1.4); Shahadah; shirk; creation; holy book; good deeds.

AO1 skills **ACTIVITIES**

How might it affect a Muslim's life believing that everything they do is being written down by the angels?

Why is Muhammad ﷺ so important to Muslims?

The next two pages will help you to:

- explore the nature of Muhammad ﷺ in relation to Islam
- assess why Muhammad ﷺ is so important to Muslims
- evaluate the attitude of Muslims towards Muhammad ﷺ.

Muhammad ﷺ and the Shahadah

A person must have declared the **Shahadah** and believe in the Shahadah to be a Muslim. The second part of the Shahadah is about believing that **Muhammad** ﷺ is the messenger of **Allah**. This signifies the position of Muhammad ﷺ in Islam. No other person or prophet before him has ever been referred to in the Shahadah, or has been regarded so highly as to be known as Habib Allah (Beloved of Allah).

Muhammad ﷺ: the seal of the prophets

Muslims believe that:

- Muhammad ﷺ is the seal (last) of the **prophets**. There will be no further prophets sent from Allah because the revelation was completed in the **Qur'an**.

- God gave the Qur'an to Muhammad ﷺ in Arabic, it was immediately written down in Arabic, and all copies are the same as the original.

- Islam did not begin with Muhammad ﷺ – it began with Adam (the first prophet), and God's message has been the same ever since.

- The Qur'an will not be distorted – the message remains unchanged so there is no need for new messengers.

- Muhammad ﷺ is the last prophet – and he is the model for all Muslims.

- Anyone who comes after Muhammad ﷺ and claims to be a prophet is not a Muslim.

Muhammad ﷺ: the model

Muhammad ﷺ, the guide for moral and spiritual development, is the key figure for all Muslims. He is the best and most excellent model of what it means to be a human being, part of Allah's creation, a **khalifah**, a prophet, a leader, a husband, a father, and most importantly, a believer.

The Shahadah in Kufic script.

AO1 skills **ACTIVITIES**

Why are so many Muslim boys named Muhammad?

AO1 skills **ACTIVITIES**

Why is Muhammad ﷺ called the 'seal of the prophets'?

> **Surah 33:21**
>
> *Ye have indeed in the Apostle of Allah a beautiful pattern (of conduct) for any one whose hope is in Allah and the Final Day, and who engages much in the Praise of Allah.*

Muslims must follow his example and be proud of him, as it says in the Qur'an:

> **Surah 68:4**
>
> *And thou (standest) on an exalted standard of character.*

Muhammad ﷺ: a human

Muhammad ﷺ was a human being: he lived, ate, drank, slept and died as all humans do. His life shows Muslims that it is possible to live a good Muslim life worshipping Allah:

> **from Surah 9:128**
>
> *Now hath come unto you an Apostle from amongst yourselves.*

The obligation to love Muhammad ﷺ

The Qur'an states that it is essential that a Muslim who claims to love Allah also loves Allah's Prophet. Muhammad ﷺ was asked to remind the ummah about this:

> **Surah 3:31**
>
> *Say: 'If ye do love Allah, Follow me: Allah will love you and forgive you your sins: For Allah is Oft-Forgiving, Most Merciful'*

It is an obligation for Muslims to love the Prophet ﷺ, because loving him is a sign of Muslim belief. One **Hadith** (collected sayings of Muhammad ﷺ) relates that perfection of faith is through love of the Prophet ﷺ:

> **Hadith**
>
> *The Prophet ﷺ said: 'None of you believes until he loves me more than he loves his children, his parents, and all people.' In the Hadith of Bukhari he said: 'None of you believes until he loves me more than he loves himself.'*

An obligation to send peace and blessings upon the Prophet

The Qur'an orders Muslims to send peace and blessings upon the Prophet ﷺ. The following verse means that Allah and the angels of Allah are constantly praising Muhammad ﷺ:

> **Surah 33:56**
>
> *Allah and His angels send blessings on the Prophet: O ye that believe! Send ye blessings on him, and salute him with all respect.*

FOR DEBATE

Does Muhammad's ﷺ perfection make it easier or harder for a Muslim to try to follow his example?

AO1+ AO2 skills **ACTIVITIES**

Choose someone who is very important to you and design a poster on 'My Hero'. Include details of who they are, why they are so special and why you look up to them. Share your work with the class and explain your poster.

How difficult would it be for you to love someone more than, for example, your parents? Can you imagine a conflict between these loves?

Who was Muhammad ?

The next two pages will help you to:

- explore the life of Muhammad ﷺ
- evaluate the nature of Muhammad ﷺ and the way in which he worshipped.

Birth of Muhammad ﷺ

According to one **Hadith**, **Muhammad** ﷺ was born into the noblest family among the Arabs. It was narrated by Al-Abbas that the Messenger of **Allah** said:

> ### Hadith
>
> *Allah created mankind, and made me from the best of them, from the best of their two groups. Then He chose tribes and made me from the best tribe. Then He chose families and made me from the best family. So I am the best of them from the best family.*

Muhammad ﷺ was born in the city of Makkah around 570 CE. His father had died before he was born and, as was the custom, his mother Amina sent him with Halima (a Bedouin woman) to the desert where he would be raised in a clean, pure environment.

When he was six he returned to his mother but she died later that year. Now an orphan, Muhammad ﷺ was left in the devout hands of his 80-year-old grandfather. After two years his grandfather also passed away, leaving him in the care of his uncle Abu Talib.

Early life

Even before prophethood Muhammad ﷺ was given titles such as Al Amin (trustworthy and honest). He was well known for his truthful nature, so much so that on one occasion he saved many of the Makkan leaders from engaging in tribal war.

ACTIVITIES

What do you understand by the term 'prophet'?

During the renovation of the Ka'bah (at the grand mosque in Makkah), the black stone had to be put back into place. Due to the nature and honour of the black stone, all the leaders of the four tribes of Makkah argued as to who would place it into the Ka'bah. This dispute continued until they agreed that the next person to walk through the gates would decide what would happen.

At this point Muhammad ﷺ walked through the gates. All the leaders were pleased (as he was Al Amin) and Muhammad ﷺ was told about the dispute. He lay his cloak down, put the black stone on the cloak and asked each of the four leaders to hold a corner while he placed it back into position. This resolved the dispute and enabled the four leaders to be pleased with the outcome.

Worship and seclusion

As a child, instead of playing with the local children, Muhammad ﷺ would often be alone, contemplating on a higher being. As he grew older, he began to see that corruption, exploitation, greed and a lack of compassion increasingly overcame the people of Makkah. The oppressed were left eagerly worshipping idols in the hope of salvation.

This state of things led Muhammad ﷺ to search for the truth. He would often visit caves and remain there in seclusion to find solitude and peace. Each year he visited the caves during what is now known as the month of **Ramadan**. These periods of isolation could last for up to 40 days as Muhammad ﷺ worshipped Allah, drawing himself closer to God.

Revelation at 40

At the age of 40, during Ramadan in the year 610 CE, Muhammad ﷺ had his first revelation. The night of this revelation is now known as Laylat-ul-Qadr (the Night of Power).

As usual Muhammad ﷺ had gone alone to the cave of Hira on Mount Nur (hill of light) to worship. At this point he heard a voice calling him to 'read' or 'proclaim'. Muhammad ﷺ was illiterate, so could not read. The angel Jibril appeared and repeated the same instruction three times. Muhammad ﷺ responded each time that he could not read. He then felt an embrace which was so tight that he felt he would die.

Suddenly, Muhammad ﷺ felt his heart see the words and was able to utter and recite them repeatedly. This was the beginning of what is now known as the Miracle and Words of Allah – the **Qur'an**.

The cave of Hira – the site of Muhammad's ﷺ first revelation.

RESEARCH NOTE

Find out more about Muhammad's ﷺ life as a young man, before his first revelation.

AO1 skills **ACTIVITIES**

Write a short biography of Muhammad's ﷺ life.

Why do you think the night of the first revelation was called the 'Night of Power'?

Why do you think Muhammad ﷺ needed seclusion in order to learn the truth?

> Surah 96:1–3
>
> *Proclaim! (or read!) in the name of thy Lord and Cherisher, Who created –*
> *Created man, out of a (mere) clot of congealed blood:*
> *Proclaim! And thy Lord is Most Bountiful*

Why is the Hijrah so important to Muslims?

The next two pages will help you to:

- explore why the Hijrah was so necessary
- evaluate the meaning and importance of Hijrah
- make links between the Hijrah and an important journey in your own life.

The gate to the Prophet's Mosque in al-Madinah.

Hijrah

Hijrah means 'emigration' or 'departure' and it is the term used to describe **Muhammad**'s migration in 622 CE from Makkah to Yathrib (now known as al-Madinah). The Hijrah is significant because it marks the beginning of the Muslim calendar. The Islamic Calendar begins after 622 CE, and each year is 11 days shorter than the Gregorian calendar so the year 2008–2009 CE is 1429 (AH) in the Muslim calendar. It is more than 1400 years since the Hijrah.

RESEARCH NOTE

What is the Gregorian calendar? How is it different from the Muslim calendar?

From Makkah to Yathrib

In Makkah, Muhammad's ﷺ preaching became widely known and because of this the city's leaders perceived him as a threat. Some of them became angry towards Muhammad ﷺ and wanted to make him stop. They became increasingly worried that his preaching would affect their trade, which relied upon pilgrims coming to worship the idols in Makkah. Muhammad's ﷺ teaching of the Oneness of God was turning people away from idol worship.

After much persecution, Muhammad's life ﷺ was increasingly threatened and some leaders wanted him killed. At the same time, the tribes and their leaders in Yathrib wanted him to join them in their city. Muhammad ﷺ left Makkah secretly and headed to Yathrib. This migration is called the Hijrah.

Arrival into Yathrib

For the Muslims of Yathrib, Muhammad's ﷺ arrival was a much celebrated event. Many were absolutely delighted that the Prophet ﷺ had decided to come to their city; they sang and welcomed him with joy.

Muhammad's ﷺ followers built the Masjid Quba (mosque) just outside Yathrib, where he stayed until he had a permanent home.

On his arrival, many of the people of Yathrib offered him a home. He was a kind and generous man, and he did not want to cause any offence or sadness among the people welcoming him by choosing one above others, so allowed his camel to make the decision for him.

The camel walked around until it finally stopped and knelt down to the ground in front of the house of Abu Ayyub. Later, Muhammad ﷺ acquired land to build a mosque in Yathrib and this became known as the al-Nabawi (Prophet's) mosque.

Some pilgrims visit these mosques while on **Hajj** or umrah (lesser pilgrimage).

Ruling in Yathrib

As Yathrib grew to be a Muslim city, the Prophet ﷺ was established as the city's ruler. He was like no other ruler, as he chose to live among the people and lived the simplest of lives. He lived with his family, involved himself with duties like everyone else, and carried out daily activities.

Other rulers did not live like this, and he became known for his belief in and practice of equality. His life became the example by which all tribes, peoples and religions could live in harmony.

Al-Madinah: the city of the prophet

Yathrib became known as the city of light. Muhammad ﷺ named the city Madinah tun Nabi (the city of the Prophet), and it is now known as al-Madinah. Millions of Muslims visit al-Madinah while on Hajj or umrah. They visit the places where Muhammad ﷺ lived, as well as the Prophet's Mosque and his burial place.

RESEARCH NOTE

Find out more about the Hijrah and those who accompanied Muhammad ﷺ on his journey.

FOR DEBATE

Do you think that different treatment of men and women in Islam suggests the message of equality has been distorted?

AO1 skills **ACTIVITIES**

Explain what Muhammad ﷺ did to change the lives of people in al-Madinah.

How was Islam established?

The next two pages will help you to:

- examine how Islam was established
- explore the ways in which Islam spread
- evaluate the nature of the Islamic state.

Old al-Madinah.

The first Islamic state

The first Islamic state was established in the city of al-Madinah (originally called Yathrib). It gave to the people who lived there equality and rights which they had not enjoyed before. In this Islamic state there was no distinction between the ruler **Muhammad** ﷺ and the citizens of al-Madinah. They were given equal rights as, according to Islam, only **Allah** could judge a person, according to their heart. Muslims were united in their worship of the Oneness of God – Allah:

> **Surah 39:14**
> *Verily the most honoured of you in the sight of Allah is (he who is) the most righteous of you.*

AO1 skills ACTIVITIES

Discuss something you have established in your own life (club, friendship or hobby). How did you get it started? How important was (is) it to you?

Return to Makkah

Even though Muhammad ﷺ had made the **Hijrah** to al-Madinah he was not left in peace. The Makkan leaders still wished to cause him harm, so they began to persecute the Muslims who had been left behind in Makkah.

In 624 CE the Battle of Badr took place. The Makkan leaders came to the town of Badr with an army of 1000 men, intending to wage war against the Muslims. The Makkan leaders left in shock, defeated by the Muslim army of only 313 men. The Muslim victory carried an important message to the Makkans – that the Muslims were different from other people, because they were so strengthened by their belief in the Oneness of God.

In 630 CE, after many other battles and broken treaties, Muhammad ﷺ returned to Makkah. He went to Makkah with an army of 10,000 men. Without any blood being shed, he entered the city of Makkah, performed tawaf (circling the Ka'bah seven times) and then called everyone to midday prayers. No one could resist Muhammad ﷺ or the Muslim army, so Makkah was declared a Muslim state.

Soon after, the people of Makkah submitted to Islam and became Muslims.

The farewell

In 632 CE the prophet knew that he would soon die. He went on a pilgrimage with about 140,000 people; this was to be his final **Hajj**. Standing at the Mount of Mercy he delivered his last sermon. He addressed the people with a powerful and emotional speech, at the end of which he cried: 'Have I fulfilled my mission?' The crowd roared with approval and testified that he had fulfilled it.

The last revelation given to Muhammad ﷺ confirms the closure of his mission and revealed the message of Islam as a way of life:

> **Surah 5:3**
>
> *This day have I perfected your religion for you, completed My favour upon you, and have chosen for you Islam as your religion.*

Muhammad's ﷺ death

When Muhammad ﷺ returned to al-Madinah he became ill with a fever, from which tradition says that he died. It is believed that he died on 8 June 632 CE (12 Rabi al-Awwal 11 AH) at the age of 63.

The death of Muhammad ﷺ was a painful and sad time for all Muslims. However, Abu Bakr, Muhammad's ﷺ close friend, companion and father-in-law, reminded them that he was a prophet who lived and died, and that Muslims worship Allah who is alive and never dies. He quoted the following verse to remind Muslims of Muhammad's ﷺ status, to help them to bring themselves together:

> **Surah 3:144**
>
> *Muhammad ﷺ is no more than an apostle: many Were the apostles that passed away before him. If he died or were slain, will ye then Turn back on your heels?*

Establishment of Islam

During the Middle Ages (about 650 to 1200 CE), Islam became the super power of its time. Its influence had spread far and wide, even reaching Spain. The Spanish province of Andalucía had been conquered by Muslims and was ruled as an Islamic state. Muhammad's ﷺ teaching of kindness and compassion had led to the establishment of Islam in many states. The concepts of justice, peace and equality regardless of race, religion, class or background, appealed to many people, making it easy to spread Islam and establish Islamic states.

RESEARCH NOTE

Research the Battle of Badr. How did the Muslim army beat the Makkan army which was three times bigger?

ACTIVITIES

AO1+ AO2 skills

Draw a timeline showing the most important events in Muhammad's ﷺ life, and explain their significance.

Imagine you are ruled by a tyrant and do not enjoy any rights. Describe the likely impact of the message of Islam on you and your family.

What are the Five Pillars of Islam?

The next two pages will help you to:

- identify the Five Pillars of Islam
- explore what Islam is built upon
- make links between the Five Pillars of Islam and practices that support you in your own life.

A zakah box.

The Five Pillars of Islam

Every male and female Muslim who has reached the age of puberty is required to perform the **Five Pillars of Islam**. They must follow these in order to fulfil their obligations to the One and Only God – **Allah**.

Hadith

On the authority of Abu 'Abd al-Rahman 'Abdullah bin 'Umar bin al-Khattab (radiyallahu 'anhuma), who said: 'I heard the Messenger of Allah, say: "Islam has been built upon five things – on testifying that there is no god save Allah, and that Muhammad is His Messenger; on performing Salah; on giving the zakah; on Hajj to the House; and on fasting during Ramadan."'

AO1 skills **ACTIVITIES**

What do you understand by this quote from the Hadith? What is Islam built upon?

Shahadah

Shahadah is the most important pillar of Islam as it is the declaration a person makes that they are a Muslim and that they believe in the One God – Allah. Simply *saying* the Shahadah does not make a person a Muslim; *having the conviction and true belief in what is said* is what makes someone a Muslim: 'There is no God but Allah and **Muhammad** ﷺ is the Messenger of Allah.'

Salah

The **Salah** are the five obligatory prayers set at different times throughout the day. This means that a Muslim lives their life around God rather than God fitting into their life (see Topic 4).

Zakah

Zakah is the purification of wealth by paying an annual tax of 2.5 per cent on accumulated assets or savings. All Muslims must pay zakah, and it is payable to a Muslim who is poor, needy or worthy of it.

Sawm

Muslims must practise **sawm** (fasting) during the holy month of **Ramadan**. Ramadan is a month of great blessings, forgiveness and saving oneself from the hellfire. Muslims must fast from dawn until sunset, abstaining from food, drink, sexual acts and committing bad deeds. Fasting is also worship, as it represents obedience and enables understanding and appreciation of what Allah gives as gifts and pleasures.

Hajj

At least once in their lifetime Muslims must do **Hajj** (pilgrimage to Makkah). This pillar applies only to those who are able, as some people may not be able to afford it or may not be well enough to do it. Historically, it could take several months or even years to travel to Makkah, but modern transport means that people can reach Makkah within a day or even hours. (See Topic 2 for more information on Hajj.)

FOR DEBATE

Discuss whether it is unrealistic to expect a person who works from 9 to 6 every day to perform Salah.

AO1 skills ACTIVITIES

Draw a spider diagram to show the five most important things in your life. How do these relate to the Five Pillars?

Summarise the Five Pillars.

Use this summary to help explain to a non-Muslim why the Five Pillars are so important to Muslims.

Does jihad mean holy war?

The next two pages will help you to:

- examine the nature of jihad
- evaluate why Muslims perform jihad
- identify the benefits of jihad for Muslims.

Jihad

Jihad is understood by Muslims to mean 'struggle'. This applies to any sort of activity someone does because of their love for **Allah**. Although jihad is a simple word, it is sometimes completely misunderstood and used incorrectly. Jihad is often understood by non-Muslims simply to mean 'holy war', but depending on the context, this may or may not be a correct usage.

There are two different types of jihad, both of which derive from the meaning of 'struggle' – greater and lesser jihad.

Greater jihad

The greater struggle is one that every Muslim man and woman encounters in their day-to-day life. All Muslims experience greater jihad, whether they live in a Muslim or non-Muslim society. The main reason for this struggle is that a Muslim's aim in life is to live according to the Prophetic **Sunnah** – to be a perfect human being, living the perfect Muslim life: 'The most excellent Jihad is that for the conquest of self' (**Hadith**).

It can be a struggle to live a good Muslim life, so every day, each Muslim faces their own jihad. Some of the daily difficulties a Muslim may face include:

- the wearing of the hijab for a Muslim woman
- waking up before sunrise to perform **Salah**
- the obligation to love and forgive someone who has hurt or insulted them
- the requirement not to cling to personal possessions, but to give in the service of others.

A Muslim woman wearing the hijab.

Lesser jihad

Unlike greater jihad, which is the personal struggle experienced by all Muslims, lesser jihad does not apply to everyone. Lesser jihad refers to the struggle by the whole community, rather than the Muslim individual, to remove evil from society.

An example of lesser jihad is where a whole community tries to remove exploitation, address underdevelopment, bridge the gap between rich and poor, and fix other problems of society.

The concept of jihad as holy war is permissible in Islam if conducted in self-defence:

Surah 2:190

Fight in the cause of Allah those who fight you, but do not transgress limits; for Allah loveth not transgressors.

Opinions on jihad

All over the world today, orthodox Muslims agree that Islamic teaching says that lesser jihad or holy war can only be called against those who threaten Islam or it can be applied in self-defence.

Islamic teaching says:

- The whole Muslim community must choose a religious leader who is renowned for his piety and religious beliefs.
- Muslims must be aware of the prospects of success otherwise it is not permissible to engage in war.
- All parties must be invited to Islam and be offered peace before any war.
- All soldiers must be faithful Muslims who are knowledgeable in the teaching of Islam and have clear understanding of the rules and regulations of the war.

Martyrs

Islam teaches that shahida (martyrs) will enter paradise without waiting for Judgement:

Surah 3:169

Think not of those who are slain in Allah's way as dead. Nay, they live, finding their sustenance in the presence of their Lord.

MUST THINK ABOUT!

What is your own jihad (personal struggle)?

RESEARCH NOTE

Research how jihad is portrayed in the media.

ACTIVITIES

What are the benefits of jihad to Muslims?

According to Islam, is it permissible to fight on behalf of those who cannot fight for themselves?

Copy the following quotes and sort them into three categories: greater jihad; lesser jihad; not jihad.

- We must fight to convert everyone to Islam.
- A man attacked my wife so I hit him.
- I love eating so I find it very difficult to fast all day in Ramadan ... but I do try.
- I live in a Muslim country and my home is under threat of invasion so I defend my property.
- I am a new Muslim convert, but I find it so hard to wear the hijab.
- Praying five times a day every day is not easy.

How do beliefs affect the lifestyles and outlooks of Muslims in the modern world?

The next two pages will help you to:

- explain the role of Islam in the modern world
- evaluate the significance of Islamic belief in relation to lifestyles and outlooks of modern Muslims.

ACTIVITIES

In pairs, discuss the role of Islam in the modern world.

Islam today

The teachings of Islam (the **Qur'an** and **Sunnah**) remain exactly the same as they were 1400 years ago. They remain as relevant today as they were then and they are practised all over the world by millions of Muslims.

The **Hadith**, which are collections of sayings or narrations of the Prophet's life, are also a source of guidance to Muslims. The Hadith were collected by the Prophet's family, household and close companions. The rank of each Hadith is dependent on the authority or reliability of the source. This is because all the Hadith were passed on by word of mouth through a chain of authority. Today Muslims can find all Hadith written and compiled according to their authority, which they can use to help guide them in modern day life.

Living with the Qur'an

No matter what age or era, the Qur'an is a message for Muslims for all times and does not require modernisation. Muslims must adhere to the teachings of the Qur'an in order to live a life of peace and tranquillity. Aspects of a Muslim's lifestyle can be modernised, but must still allow them to live according to the Islamic principles laid down by the Qur'an:

> **Surah 5:3**
> *This day have I perfected your religion for you, completed My favour upon you, and have chosen for you Islam as your religion.*

The Sunnah

Although the body of **Muhammad** ﷺ is dead, his message and soul live on through the Qur'an and Hadith. Muslims can obtain everything by following in his footsteps and modelling his practices, by living by the Sunnah.

A Muslim reading the Qur'an.

The modern world requires a Muslim to look deeply at the essence of Muhammad ﷺ; to focus and acquaint themselves with his lifestyle and attributes, and to practise what he set as a way of life – spreading love and peace among the world, as he was known as rahmatul al Alameen (mercy to the world). **Allah** says:

> **Surah 21:107**
> *We sent thee not, but as a Mercy for all creatures.*

The Qur'an also says:

> **Surah 59:7**
> *So take what the Apostle assigns to you, and deny yourselves that which he withholds from you.*

Modern life and the Five Pillars

Muslims can certainly live by the **Shahadah** in the modern world. This is demonstrated by the millions of people who are Muslims and who confirm their belief in the Shahadah.

Although it may seem difficult to perform **Salah** in the modern world, nevertheless it is possible. Most employers provide a multi-faith room to cater for all religious worship, including the Muslim Salah. The Salah usually fits quite well during breaks or lunch time, so inconvenience and lack of appropriate facilities are not excuses for a modern working Muslim not to perform Salah.

It is more necessary than ever to perform **zakah** as there is so much poverty and many people in need.

Modern life does not stop a Muslim from practising **sawm**; in fact, it actually helps a Muslim have a better understanding of poverty and need.

The modern world has made **Hajj** more accessible and comfortable than it would previously have been for many people: travel times are shorter and air-conditioning helps overcome the heat. It has made it possible for those for whom it would have been impossible, such as the weak or disabled. It is no longer a struggle to complete Hajj, although the pilgrim needs patience as there are usually millions of people doing the same thing at the same time.

Modern life and Islam

Whether the modern world makes it easier or harder for someone to live as a Muslim depends on the individual and how they respond to the world around them. Islam does not interfere with modernity and allows all Muslims to work, live and integrate with other communities. It encourages each individual to benefit themselves and others with knowledge, skills and independence.

FOR DEBATE

Doing Hajj 100 years ago was better than it is now because you had more time to contemplate the purpose of doing Hajj and to prepare for it.

AO1 skills ACTIVITIES

Design a rulebook for Muslims in the modern world. Include a list of *Do*s and *Don't*s. You could consider whether, in the modern world, Muslims are allowed to drink alcohol, have sex before marriage, commit adultery or steal, and whether they should still perform Salah, respect their parents, eat halal meat (meat that is prepared in a particular way that is acceptable to Islam), or go on Hajj. Give reasons for your *Do*s and *Don't*s.

Modern Muslim men.

Welcome to the Grade Studio

GCSE is about what you can do, not what you can't do. You need to know what examiners want in your answers so you can get the best possible marks. In GCSE Religious Studies there are two things that examiners are looking for. These are called assessment objectives (AO). Questions are designed to help examiners find out how well you do in each assessment objective.

Graded examples for this topic

AO1

AO1 questions test what you know and how well you can explain and analyse things. Let's look at an AO1 question to see what examiners expect you to do.

Question

Explain what you understand by the message of Islam. **[6 marks]**

Possible steps to answer the question: *What should an answer be like and how do examiners work out what is a good response or a poor one?*

Examiners use levels to measure the responses, and award marks accordingly (AO1 questions are worth 6 marks). There are three levels for AO1. A good answer will not only give a definition, it will explain in some detail what it means, how it links to other beliefs and how it affects a Muslim's life. You could build an answer like this:

Student's answer

The message of Islam is part of the core belief that a Muslim must believe and practise. Muslims believe that God sent the message to humans so that they can live a good life on earth and have an eternal life in the afterlife.

This could refer to the angels, holy books or prophets, which were sent by Allah to teach humans how to live life. Muslims must believe in all the angels, holy books and prophets as this is part of their core belief. This means that they have to follow Muhammad (PBUH) as he was the last and final messenger. They must also practise the Five Pillars of Islam, which are Shahadah, prayer, fasting, zakah and performing Hajj. This is so they can be good Muslims.

The message of Islam is belief that Allah is One and The Only. Muslims have to believe that 'There is no God but Allah and that Muhammad (PBUH) is the messenger of God'. This is called the Shahadah. Muslims live their lives by this declaration. For example, when a baby is born the father whispers the call to prayer in the baby's ear, and when someone is dying it is recommended they utter it at the point of death.

Examiner's comment

The student gave a basic overview of their understanding of the question with no use of specialist terms or enough detail. (Level 1)

The student then moved on to explain further, giving some relevant examples and using some specialist terms. (Level 2)

Addition of an explanation using detailed analysis which shows complete understanding of the question and includes significant and appropriate specialist terms presented in a structured format brings the answer to *Level 3*.

Question

'It is not easy to believe and practise Islam in the modern world.' Discuss this statement. You should include different, supported points of view and a personal viewpoint. You must refer to Islam in your answer. **[12 marks]**

AO2

AO2 questions try to test your ability to present more than one point of view and to evaluate them. Again, examiners use levels to measure the quality of your response, and award marks accordingly (up to 12 marks for AO2 questions). A good answer will not only state a point of view, it will justify that view in some detail, drawing on religious beliefs and teachings.

Student's answer

I disagree because there are millions of Muslims today who believe and practise Islam. It may be hard for some Muslims because they have to work and may find it difficult to pray or for a woman to wear the veil. Nevertheless, I think the majority still find ways to fit their lifestyle around Islam.

Examiner's comment

The student gave their opinion and gave a reason for their view. (*Level 1*) The student then moved on to give good examples to support their answer and referred to another viewpoint. (*Level 2*)

A *Level 3* answer would have to explain both points of view in more detail, referring to religious or moral ideas about the statement and give a personal response.

A *Level 4* answer would need to discuss thoroughly the idea of Muslim beliefs and practices in the modern world, consider different views and include a supported personal response.

Student's improved answer

I disagree because there are millions of Muslims today who believe and practise Islam.

It may be hard for some Muslims because they have to work and may find it difficult to pray or for a woman to wear the veil. Nevertheless, I think the majority still find ways to fit their lifestyle around Islam.

A Muslim response to this statement would be that much of the core belief in Islam is down to faith and belief in the Oneness of God, his messages via the angels, holy books and the prophets. This is easy to practise in the modern world. Practising the Five Pillars of Islam might pose some difficulty, but it is possible to do this and live a modern lifestyle at the same time. Performing Salah might be the biggest challenge, especially for workers, but now more employers are more than happy to offer prayer rooms.

However, some Muslims may disagree with this viewpoint. They may argue that practices such as wearing the veil and praying are difficult to fit into the modern world. These things are hard to do, so it is not easy to practise Islam in the modern world.

I think that some Muslims do genuinely find it hard to practise Islam today. If you want to be a Muslim then it is your choice, so society should accept your decision and help make it easy for you. Modernity should not affect religion; this is just an excuse for some Muslims who want to live modern lifestyles. For example, I have a Muslim friend Imran who doesn't pray, not because it is hard but because he is lazy.

These specimen answers provide an outline of how you could construct your response. Space does not allow us to give a full response. The examiner will be looking for more detail in your actual exam responses.

Remember and Reflect

AO1 Describe, explain and analyse, using knowledge and understanding

Find the answer on:

1 Explain, in one sentence, what each of the following Key words means:
  a Allah
  b tawhid
  c shirk
  d prophet
  e Shahadah
  f Salah
  g sawm
  h zakah
  i Hajj

PAGE 5

2 Name two facts about the Ninety-Nine Names of Allah. PAGE 6

3 Describe the nature and functions of angels. PAGE 9

4 How many angels are there? PAGE 9

5 How many holy books were sent by God, and to whom? PAGE 9

6 Explain Muslim understanding about the Qur'an. PAGE 9

7 What do Muslims believe about Jesus? PAGE 9

8 What do Muslims believe is the purpose of life? PAGE 10

9 Outline the different stages of the afterlife. PAGE 11

10 Explain the meaning of the 'Seal of Prophets'. PAGE 12

11 What happened to Muhammad's ﷺ parents? PAGE 14

12 Why is the Hijrah so important to Muslims? PAGE 16

13 Explain what the Five Pillars of Islam are. PAGE 20

AO2 Use evidence and reasoned argument to express and evaluate personal responses, informed insights, and differing viewpoints

1 Why do people believe in God? Explain your answer.

2 Analyse whether following the beliefs of a religious figure would enable you to be a good-natured human being.

3 Do you believe in heaven and hell? Why or why not? Relate your answer to a Muslim viewpoint.

4 What are the essential things a Muslim must believe? Why are they essential to Muslim belief?

5 Muslims must find it difficult to practise Islam in the modern world. True or false?

6 Copy out the table. As well as entering Key points add any other notes you think relevant, and give your personal response with reasons.

Core belief	Key points	What I think and why
Allah – the One and Only		
The last prophet – Muhammad ﷺ		
Model life of Muhammad ﷺ		
Five Pillars of Islam		

Topic 2: Special days and pilgrimage

The Big Picture

In this Topic you will be exploring the nature of Muslim special days and pilgrimages. You will understand the importance of:

- Ramadan
- Id-ul Fitr, Id-ul-Adha, Salat-ul-Jumu'ah, Mawlid an-Nabi
- Hajj.

You will also consider the significance of these times for Muslims as individuals and communities, as well as the role pilgrimages might play in the spiritual development of Muslims.

What?

You will:

- understand how and why the special days came into being
- understand what the Hajj is and why it is important to Muslims
- understand how the Hajj is used in Islam as a source of belief and practice.

How?

By:

- examining the origins and nature of the special days and the Hajj
- understanding the importance of the special days and the Hajj
- evaluating your own views about the role and importance of pilgrimages and celebrations.

Why?

Because:

- it is important to understand the place of special days and the Hajj in Islam and its influence on the beliefs and practices of Muslims
- Muslims regard the Hajj as one of the Five Pillars of Islam.

GET STARTED

Look at the pictures. Do you think that celebrations are spoilt by commercialism?

What might someone going to an event such as the Glastonbury festival and someone going on a pilgrimage have in common? What might be different about these journeys and their purposes?

In what ways might life itself be like a pilgrimage? Give reasons for your answers.

Special days and pilgrimage

KEY INFORMATION

- Many of the world's great religions have a place or places they encourage people to visit on pilgrimage.

- A place of pilgrimage may give information about the history of the religion, including the life of the founder and other key figures.

- The main beliefs and teachings about how people should live may be demonstrated by going on pilgrimage.

- The Hajj is the key pilgrimage of Islam, where a Muslim visits Makkah as part of the Five Pillars of Islam.

- The festival of Id-ul-Adha is celebrated on the tenth day of Dhul-Hijjah, the month of the Hajj.

- The fasting month of Ramadan is important to the development of Muslims' appreciation of Allah's blessings, through contemplation of the Qur'an and the exercise of self-control.

- The festival of Id-ul-Fitr is celebrated at the end of Ramadan.

- The festival of Mawlid an-Nabi is a celebration of the Prophet Muhammad's ﷺ birthday which is honoured by some Muslims but not by all.

KEY QUESTIONS

KNOWLEDGE AND UNDERSTANDING

Why is the Hajj so important to Muslims?

What does it help Muslims to achieve?

What attitudes should a person on the Hajj have?

Why is Id-ul-Adha so important to Muslims?

Why is Id-ul-Fitr so important to Muslims?

ANALYSIS AND EVALUATION

How can visiting places that were important over 1400 years ago be important today?

Why do different groups of Muslims treat the birthday of the Prophet Muhammad ﷺ differently?

Why don't all Muslims believe the same things about special days and pilgrimages if they all use the same holy book, the Qur'an?

Arafat A plain, 14 km from Makkah, where pilgrims gather to worship, as part of the Hajj.

Hadith A collection of sayings of the Prophet Muhammad ﷺ which Muslims consult to help guide them in their understanding.

Hajj Annual pilgrimage to Makkah, which each Muslim must undertake at least once in their lifetime if he or she has the health and wealth to do so. One of the Five Pillars of Islam.

Ibrahim A prophet of Allah.

ihram The simple clothing of a pilgrim on Hajj; also the state in which the individual performs Hajj.

Isma'il The son of Ibrahim and Hajar, whom Allah asked Ibrahim to sacrifice, but was then saved by Allah.

Ka'bah Cube-shaped structure in the centre of the grand mosque in Makkah. It was built by Ibrahim and was cleansed of idols by the Prophet Muhammad ﷺ. Muslims pray in the direction of this building.

Makkah The city where the Prophet Muhammad ﷺ was born.

Mina A place near Makkah where pilgrims stay during 10–12 Dhul-Hijjah and perform some of the activities of the Hajj.

Qur'an Allah's word revealed through Muhammad ﷺ to humanity; the most important holy book of Islam.

Ramadan The ninth month of the Islamic calendar during which fasting is required from just before dawn until sunset as ordered by Allah in the Qur'an.

Safa and Marwah Two hills in Makkah between which Hajar ran to search for water for Isma'il. Walking or running between these hills is part of the Hajj.

sa'y The practice of walking or hastening between the hills Safa and Marwah as part of the Hajj, symbolising Hajar's search for water.

tawaf Circling the Ka'bah seven times in an anti-clockwise direction in worship of Allah, performed as part of the Hajj.

ummah Worldwide community of Muslims; the nation of Islam.

wudu Ritual washing before praying.

FOR INTEREST The Hajj is one of the Five Pillars of Islam or duties that a Muslim should try to achieve in their lifetime. It should be not just a physical journey to the places linked to the revelations to the Prophet Muhammad ﷺ but should also be about an inner, spiritual journey.

How special can a journey be? Do you have a journey which is special to you? What is it and why? Compare examples in your class or group. What kinds of journey have people chosen? Are any of them religious journeys?

Pilgrims on Hajj.

Teenagers on a hiking trip.

Why do Muslims celebrate Salat-ul-Jumu'ah?

The next two pages will help you to:

- identify the important parts of Salat-ul-Jumu'ah
- examine how Salat-ul-Jumu'ah reflects Muslim belief
- evaluate the importance of prayer to Muslims.

Muslims gathered in a mosque for prayer on a Friday.

Prayer

Prayer is very important to religious people. It can serve a number of purposes, such as allowing a believer to thank their God for a blessing or to ask for something that they feel needs to happen. It may be used as an opportunity to ask for forgiveness if they realise they have upset someone or their God by their actions. For Muslims, prayers can be carried out in private at home or in the office but it is also important that they come together to pray with others.

Salah is the name for the prayers that Muslims must perform five times each day, and is one of the Five Pillars. This follows Allah's commandment to Muhammad ﷺ, following the Prophet's ﷺ night journey to heaven. Muslim children as young as seven are encouraged to pray five times a day.

Performing Salah is not only a spiritual duty to Allah but it also shows that each Muslim is part of a community of faith, which is particularly important when praying in a mosque. Prayer is something which involves the whole of the person – body, mind and spirit.

Muslims can pray anywhere which is clean. Before they pray, they must perform **wudu** (ritual washing) to ensure that they are cleansed. Many Muslims believe that it is very important to pray with others in a mosque. Praying together as part of the **ummah** helps Muslims to remember that all are equal in the eyes of Allah.

Salat-ul-Jumu'ah

Friday is the most important day to come together to pray in the mosque, so Salat-ul-Jumu'ah (Friday prayers) are the most important. In Arabic, *al-Jumu'ah* means 'the day of gathering', because Muslims believe that it was on this day of the week that the body of the first man, Adam, was created. Some Muslims teach that the Day of Judgement will take place on al-Jumu'ah.

A Muslim writer has suggested that a Muslim should regard this day as important as the celebration of Id-ul-Fitr.

Although al-Jumu'ah is in some ways a normal trading day, Muslims should recognise the priority and importance of prayer:

> **Surah 62:9**
>
> *O ye who believe! When the call is proclaimed to prayer on Friday (the Day of Assembly), hasten earnestly to the Remembrance of Allah, and leave off business (and traffic): That is best for you if ye but knew!*

Islam says that this should be a day of celebration, not discipline. Muslims should reflect on the special blessings that only Allah can bring to them. One Muslim writer said that going to Salat-ul-Jumu'ah was a way to make sure that you go to paradise.

According to Nasai, attendance at Salat-ul-Jumu'ah is required by all male Muslims who have reached puberty. However, the instructions to pray may be suspended in some situations, as one Muslim writer stated: 'A traveller does not have to perform salat-ul-Jumu'ah' (Sahih al-Bukhari).

> **Surah 62:10**
>
> *'And when the Prayer is finished, then may ye disperse through the land, and seek of the Bounty of Allah: and celebrate the Praises of Allah often (and without stint): that ye may prosper.'*

ACTIVITIES

Why do people pray? Think of as many reasons as you can and write a list with a partner. Share these with the class and then as a class try to order them in importance. Then examine your list again. Would this be the order that a Muslim might choose? Are there any important reasons that you have left out, especially ones that Muslims might regard as important?

AO1 skills **ACTIVITIES**

Read the quote on the left. Why do Muslims believe that following Salah might make them successful? Does this mean that prayer will guarantee you a good life?

Why do you think wudu (ritual washing) is so important? Think about the symbolic meanings it might have as well as the straightforward meaning.

Why is Ramadan important to Muslims?

Ramadan

Ramadan is the ninth month of the lunar calendar that Islam follows. The month moves on eleven or twelve days each year. Muslims believe that the sighting of a new moon should be the start of the fast, which is observed every day of the month by those who are able.

The next two pages will help you to:

- identify the important parts of Ramadan
- examine how Ramadan reflects Muslim beliefs and practices
- evaluate the importance of self-discipline and self-denial as ways in which a person may grow.

AO1 skills ACTIVITIES

Talk with a partner about the things that you would find most difficult to give up for a month, and why. Each of you has one minute to share your ideas.

A calendar showing how to observe Ramadan.

There are several reasons why it is considered important to observe Ramadan:

- The **Qur'an** was revealed by Allah sending the angel Jibril to Muhammad ﷺ during Ramadan. Ramadan is sometimes referred to as 'the month of the Qur'an'. Many Muslims try to spend more time reading it during that month in order to have a greater understanding of the will of Allah. Muslims should thank Allah for the gift of the Qur'an to the world, as this has enabled them to understand Allah's will.

- There is a tradition that the gates of heaven are unlocked and that the gates of hell are locked. This is a way of saying that a good deed during the month can bring many good consequences to the person who performs it. Muslims believe that it is also easier to do good during Ramadan as the devils of hell have been chained and are unable to tempt them away from the will of Allah. Therefore it is especially important to use the opportunities that will come during the month wisely.

- It is a time to give up some bad or unhelpful habits as an act of devotion to Allah. The discipline of giving up a habit will also help the Muslim to understand the importance of self-control. Giving up something, whether it is food, cups of tea or coffee or smoking, can be a real struggle. '*I think that Ramadan is important to me as a Muslim because I believe that it shows real commitment and faith to Islam because Ramadan is a hard thing to do each year, like Lent is for some Christians*' (Sayful Islam, 15-year-old student).

- Most Muslims will try to fast during the month of Ramadan. This is not the only time during the year when Muslims should fast, but it is the only one where those who can must fast. There are some exceptions such as the ill (both physically and mentally), the elderly, pregnant or feeding mothers, children who haven't reached puberty or those who might be travelling. Fasting is about developing self-discipline.

- During the month, Muslims will try to make sure that, as well as only eating and drinking at the times allowed, they also have better control over how long they sleep, how often they have sex and how well they use their time.

- Ramadan is a time when Muslims may have to deal with the reactions of others to their faith, and this can test their willingness to explain their faith to others. Some people in non-Muslim countries may not understand what is going on. '*It can be difficult to keep Ramadan on a school day. On a normal day, it is not. On other days, it is very difficult. I have come close to breaking point. My friends who are not Muslims have not always understood it. Sometimes they do like to tease me with food!*' (Sayful Islam).

- Ramadan is also a time when the value of belonging to the Muslim community of faith or **ummah** is strengthened, as more time is spent with family or with fellow believers in the mosque both in prayer and in the meals that start and break the daily fasts.

FOR DEBATE

What might fasting enable a Muslim to achieve that they wouldn't achieve otherwise?

AO2 skills ACTIVITIES

Write an email that a Muslim teenager might send to a friend who asks them what is the benefit in keeping the fasting of Ramadan, trying to answer this question.

Do you think you can be a good Muslim without keeping Ramadan? What might a Muslim say about this? Give reasons for your answer, showing that you have thought about it from more than one point of view.

'Self-control is one of the most valuable things a person can learn from Ramadan.' What do you think? What problems do people have who want to develop more self-control?

Why is the story of Ibrahim and Isma'il important to Muslims?

The next two pages will help you to:

- understand the story of Ibrahim and Isma'il
- be able to explain the importance of Ibrahim's trust in Allah
- evaluate the importance of obeying Allah's will.

Modern-day Mina.

The story of Ibrahim and Isma'il

Allah called **Ibrahim** to serve Him. The **Qur'an** says: 'For Allah did take Abraham for a friend' (from Surah 4:125). Ibrahim left his wealthy life in a city to go where he was told. He turned his back on the idol worship of his father's family. He would follow the One God – Allah.

Ibrahim lived with his wife Sarah. Allah had made a promise to Ibrahim that he would become a father but this seemed impossible as Sarah was unable to have children. Ibrahim had a second wife, called Hajar. Hajar was able to give Ibrahim a son. The boy's name was **Isma'il**.

AO1 skills **ACTIVITIES**

Try to think of an important story which reveals the way in which people think about the world. It could be a Greek myth or a story told by Jesus or another religious leader. Why does the story work?

Why are stories good ways of conveying ideas? Working with a partner, write a list about why stories can help people understand ideas about God and religion.

Ibrahim felt that he would be prepared to make any sacrifice that Allah asked of him. Had he not been willing to give up his life in the city and to travel in the desert?

Allah decided that Ibrahim's faith needed to be tested. One night, Allah sent Ibrahim a dream. In it, Allah asked Ibrahim to sacrifice his son Isma'il. Ibrahim woke in a sweat – he was terrified by what he was being asked to do.

He told his son about the dream. The boy looked at his father and said, 'If that is the will of Allah, we should follow it'. He looked at his father and told him not to worry but to be obedient to the call he had received. Neither father nor son could understand why Allah had asked them to do this but both resolved to do it.

So they set out to **Mina**, where the sacrifice was due to happen. On the way there, Shaytan (the Devil) appeared in disguise to try and tempt the father and son away from the will of Allah.

Shaytan first appeared to Ibrahim as a human being. Shaytan asked Ibrahim if Allah really required this sacrifice or was it his imagination? Would Allah really demand a human sacrifice – it seemed so unlikely. How could he allow himself to destroy his family as the result of a nightmare?

Then Shaytan appeared to Isma'il. Shaytan asked the boy to think about the situation – surely what his father was doing showed that he was a mad man? The sensible thing would be to run and remain safely alive.

Each time Shaytan tempted them, the family resisted.

Finally, they arrived at Mina. Ibrahim took Isma'il and lay him on the altar of sacrifice. As Ibrahim drew his knife and raised it, the voice of Allah came from heaven telling Ibrahim to stop.

The test of faith had been passed. Both were willing to do as they believed Allah was telling them to do. In Allah's great love, Allah provided a ram that was to be sacrificed in Isma'il's place.

The faith of Ibrahim was rewarded. Sarah, his childless wife, soon became pregnant and gave birth to his son, Ishaq.

Both of the sons were brought up to obey the will of Allah.

The importance of the story

This story has become the basis of many important ideas in Islam. One anonymous Islamic writer said that Ibrahim faced a number of choices:

Who should Ibrahim choose?
Love of God or Love of self?
Prophethood or Fatherhood?
Loyalty to God or Loyalty to family?
Faith or Emotion?
Truth or Reality?
Consciousness or Instinct?

Responsibility or Pleasure?
Duty or Right?
Tawhid or Shirk?
Advancing or Remaining?
To Become or To Be?
And finally, God or Isma'il?
What should Ibrahim choose?

ACTIVITIES

'The story of Ibrahim and Isma'il is barbaric.' What do you think? What might a Muslim think? Give reasons for your answers, showing that you have drawn upon Islamic belief.

What would you personally find the most difficult thing to give up if you had to? Give reasons for your answer.

Why do Muslims go on Hajj?

The next two pages will help you to:

- identify the importance of the Hajj
- examine how the Hajj reflects Muslim belief
- evaluate the importance of ihram as a way to show humility while on the Hajj.

Hajj: the journey of a lifetime

Journeys have been important to the development of religious people.

The **Hajj** or pilgrimage to **Makkah** is one of the Five Pillars of Islam, the five beliefs and actions that every believer should try to fulfil in their life.

Every Muslim who is healthy should try to make this journey at least once in their lifetime. Muslims believe that visiting the places where Muhammad ﷺ received the words of the **Qur'an** from the angel Jibril should help them better understand what their religion teaches. If a person is old or sick, disabled or poor, they are not expected to go on the Hajj.

If a person is going on the Hajj, they must ensure that any family left behind at home are cared for.

A man who completes the pilgrimage is called a *Hajji* and a woman is called a *Hajjah*.

Hajj is associated with Muhammad ﷺ but Muslims believe that the importance of Makkah goes back 4000 years, to the time of **Ibrahim**.

 **ACTIVITIES**

Write about the most important journey you have undertaken in your life. Why was it so important? If you do not think you have made an important journey, which journey would you like to make?

Share your answers with a partner and then with the class. What do the different journeys have in common? What is different about them?

The Hajj takes place over six days, 8–13 Dhul-Hijjah, during the twelfth month of the Muslim calendar. From all over the world, Muslims come together for this special time when they believe they can be blessed by Allah. There is a major international airport in Jeddah which helps to reduce the travelling time of the millions of people who make this journey. The city of Makkah has many hotels and other places for pilgrims to stay. Non-Muslims are not allowed to visit the various sites of pilgrimage in Makkah and al-Madinah at any time.

One important lesson that the pilgrims to Makkah should learn from the experience is that everyone is equal in the eyes of Allah. They should also learn to treat fellow pilgrims with respect, to see that they are treated properly as members of the worldwide community of Islam or **ummah**.

Ihram

One way of expressing this respect is the wearing of **ihram** or special clothing. Boys and men will wear two white, unsown sheets of cotton. One of these is tied around the person's waist and the other is draped across their left shoulder. The white colour emphasises that the pilgrim is trying not to boast about themselves but to seek the pure, good will of Allah. As well as the wearing of ihram, boys and men must not cover their heads.

Girls and women wear long, plain dresses and they cover their heads.

Ihram also describes the state a person must be in when on Hajj and this is achieved by following certain rules: 'Let there be no obscenity, nor wickedness, nor wrangling in the Hajj' (from Surah 2:197). Once they have begun their pilgrimage, people are not allowed to:

- Use any perfumed soap or perfume. They are there to concentrate on Allah and Allah's prophet, not to make themselves attractive to the opposite sex.
- Wear any jewellery apart from a wedding ring. Jewellery is often used as a status symbol to show someone's wealth or power.
- Kill or harm any animals or insects. All life must be valued as it comes from Allah. They also must not break or uproot plants.
- Do anything which is dishonest or arrogant. If they speak or act in such a way, then the blessings of the Hajj will not be theirs.
- Carry weapons. Any act of violence cannot be tolerated.
- Have sexual relations, as this will distract the pilgrims when they should be concentrating on Allah.
- Cut their hair or nails.
- Wear footwear that draws attention to their ankles.
- Be disobedient or carry out disputes during Hajj.
- Cover their heads (this only applies to men and boys).

ACTIVITIES

Why do Muslims believe that ihram is so important to the Hajj? Could a person still have a good Hajj without following all the instructions?

What is humility? How does the Hajj contribute to the development of a Muslim's humility?

'The idea of pilgrimage is irrelevant to the world today.' Do a survey to find out what ten people think about this statement and why. What do you think? Give your reasons.

Some things are not permitted when wearing ihram: wearing perfume and jewellery, killing animals or the carrying of weapons.

What benefits do Muslims get from the Hajj?

The next two pages will help you to:

- explain the importance of visiting Makkah
- examine how visiting the **Ka'bah** can benefit a Muslim
- evaluate the symbolism involved in the Hajj.

Visiting the Ka'bah is very important to Muslims on the Hajj. They believe that this building was built by Ibrahim and Isma'il.

Beginning the Hajj

Pilgrims arrive by coach or by aeroplane to **Makkah**. The journey will include several opportunities to pray and prepare for the pilgrimage they are embarking on.

When a person arrives in Makkah at the beginning of the **Hajj**, they are advised to make themselves comfortable at their accommodation. Then they go to the **Ka'bah**. The Ka'bah is an important building which Muslims believe was built by the prophet **Ibrahim** and his son **Isma'il**. Inside the Ka'bah is an empty space which at the time of Muhammad ﷺ was filled with idols.

The prophet was appalled by the idols and removed them, saying that this was the House of God and should not be ruined by such desecration. Some Muslims believe that the Ka'bah is immediately below the seat of Allah in heaven. It is now contained in a huge courtyard in Masjid al-Haram (the sacred mosque).

ACTIVITIES

What would you most like to change about the world? Give reasons for your answers. Share your ideas with a partner and then with the class. Create a spider diagram to show your ideas.

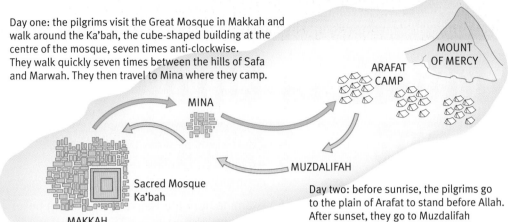

Day one: the pilgrims visit the Great Mosque in Makkah and walk around the Ka'bah, the cube-shaped building at the centre of the mosque, seven times anti-clockwise. They walk quickly seven times between the hills of Safa and Marwah. They then travel to Mina where they camp.

MOUNT OF MERCY

ARAFAT CAMP

MINA

MUZDALIFAH

Sacred Mosque Ka'bah

MAKKAH

Day two: before sunrise, the pilgrims go to the plain of Arafat to stand before Allah. After sunset, they go to Muzdalifah where they collect stones.

Day three: in the morning, the pilgrims return to Mina where they throw stones at three pillars. The pilgrimage ends with an animal sacrifice. After returning to Makkah for a final circle of the Ka'bah, the pilgrims go home or visit al-Madinah.

RESEARCH NOTE

Do some research to compare going on Hajj 100 years ago with going on Hajj now. Do you think the differences affect the benefits for the pilgrim?

Tawaf

On the first day of the Hajj (8 Dhul-Hijjah), the pilgrims will walk or run around the Ka'bah seven times in an anti-clockwise direction. This movement around the Ka'bah is called **tawaf**. As they do this, pilgrims say a prayer. Every circling of the Ka'bah begins with the pilgrim going up to the Black Stone which is set into the wall of the building, to either kiss the stone or if they cannot do this, they will raise their arms in the direction of it.

Muslims believe that this stone was sent from heaven by Allah. The pilgrim must try to concentrate their thoughts on Allah and Allah's blessings while they perform tawaf otherwise their tawaf is pointless.

The Ka'bah is usually covered with a large black cloth. When the pilgrimage comes to an end, the cloth is cut into small pieces for the pilgrims. These are a physical reminder of what they have seen and experienced. The pilgrims will keep it in a place of honour at home when they return.

Safa and Marwah

After they have walked around the Ka'bah, the pilgrims walk seven times between the two hills of **Safa** and **Marwah**. This practice is called **sa'y**, and it reminds people of the story of Hajar, Ibrahim's wife, who had to run between the two hills to fetch water for her baby Isma'il. These hills are now joined by a tunnel walkway which was designed to make it safer for pilgrims to walk between them.

Having performed sa'y, the pilgrims have completed Umrat al-tammatu. Umrah (lesser pilgrimage) itself can be performed at any time of the year. The pilgrims then journey to **Mina**, to be ready for the next stage of the Hajj.

ACTIVITIES

Write a paragraph explaining why the Ka'bah is such an important building in Islam.

How might a person who has been able to make the Hajj feel or think differently about their faith?

'Realistically you will not understand what it truly means to be a Muslim until you have been on Hajj.' Do you agree? What might a Muslim say? Refer to Muslim teachings in your answers. Make sure that you have considered a variety of views.

Pilgrims moving between Safa and Marwah.

Why do Muslims think the Hajj is about defeating evil?

A Muslim story about pilgrimage

There is a Muslim story that a man once set out to go on the **Hajj** but on his journeying to **Makkah**, he met an old, poor woman so he gave her all his money and food. He had to return home, unable to pay for his travel to Makkah. However, many of his friends said that he had made a good Hajj as they had seen in a vision Allah blessing their generous friend who had put the needs of others above his own.

The next two pages will help you to:

- explain why Muslims regard the confrontation of evil as so important
- examine how the Hajj reflects Muslim belief about the defeat of evil
- evaluate how the Hajj reinforces the idea of the ummah, the community of faith in Islam.

Pilgrims throwing stones at the pillars at Mina.

Pilgrimage is not just about a literal journey but is about the pilgrim's mental attitude before and after the actual trip. This is where the Hajj plays an important role in confronting evil.

Arafat

The next morning, on 9 Dhul-Hijjah (the month of the pilgrimage), the pilgrims leave **Mina** for the plain of **Arafat**. They stand at Arafat and think about the message of the last sermon preached by the Prophet Muhammad ﷺ. For all pilgrims, this is the highlight of the Hajj. Pilgrims must spend the afternoon on the plain of Arafat until after sunset. Many pilgrims spend time praying and thinking about the direction their lives are taking. It is compulsory to spend some time at Arafat in order to have made the Hajj.

When the sun sets, the pilgrims leave Arafat for Muzdalifah which is between Arafat and Mina. Here the pilgrims gather 49 pebbles for the rituals they will perform on the following days. Many pilgrims spend the night sleeping on the ground at Muzdalifah before returning to Mina the following day for the next stage of the Hajj.

This is now the 10 Dhul-Hijjah and, for Muslims not on Hajj, the beginning of Id-ul-Adha, one of the most important festivals in Islam (see Topic 2.8).

Mina: stoning the Devil

The rejection of evil is central to many of the world's religions and in Islam it is expressed physically during the Hajj. This rejection of evil starts at Mina on the third day of the Hajj (10 Dhul-Hijjah).

At Mina the pilgrims perform a ritual known as rami al-jamarat. This is where the pilgrims throw stones at three large pillars to signify their rejection of the Devil and the evil the Devil tries to bring into the world. This reminds the pilgrims of the trials experienced by **Ibrahim** while he decided whether to sacrifice his son as demanded by Allah. The Devil challenged him three times, and each time Ibrahim refused to give in to temptation. Each pillar marks the location of one place where Ibrahim rejected the Devil.

On the first day when rami al-jamarat is performed, pilgrims stone the largest pillar known as Jamarat al-Aqabah. On the second and third days, all three are stoned. The stoning consists of throwing seven pebbles each time. The stoning signifies that the pilgrims will pursue the way of Allah at all costs, and not the way of the Devil.

FOR DEBATE

Can you go on a pilgrimage without actually arriving at the place you were supposed to be going to?

AO1 skills ACTIVITIES

What do you think of as evil?

Write a list of activities or thoughts you think are evil. Why do you think this?

Is evil something that we are taught to be aware of by our school, parents or society? Do we need a sense of something being evil to understand that other things can be good?

AO2 skills ACTIVITIES

Stoning the pillars at Mina is very important as it shows the commitment of Muslims to get rid of evil from the world. What would you describe as evil? What do you think causes it? Can it be prevented? Give reasons for your answer, referring to Islamic teaching.

'The only thing necessary for the triumph of evil is for good people to do nothing' (Edmund Burke). Do you agree with Burke? Explain how a Muslim might respond to it. Give reasons for your answer.

How does the Hajj end?

The next two pages will help you to:

- identify how the Hajj is both a physical and spiritual journey
- evaluate the long-term effects making Hajj should have on a Muslim.

An animal being slaughtered on the tenth day of Dhul-Hijjah.

Sacrifice

After the stoning of the Devil, an animal is sacrificed. This commemorates the ram given to **Ibrahim** by Allah so that he did not have to sacrifice his son **Isma'il** (see Topic 2.3).

In the past, the pilgrims slaughtered the animal themselves or supervised the slaughtering. Today, many pilgrims can buy a sacrifice voucher in **Makkah** before the **Hajj** begins, which allows an animal to be slaughtered in their name on the tenth of the month, without the pilgrim having to be there when it happens. There are butchers who will sacrifice for each pilgrim. A cow can be an effective sacrifice for seven people. The meat is packaged and given to charity and sent to poor people around the world.

 REMEMBER THIS

The Hijrah is the term used to describe Muhammad's ﷺ migration from Makkah to al-Madinah (see Topic 1.6).

The last days of the Hajj

On this day or the next (10 or 11 Dhul-Hijjah), the pilgrims return to the Masjid al-Haram in Makkah to perform another **tawaf** – the Tawaf az-Ziyarah or Tawaf al-Ifadah, which again involves circling the **Ka'bah** seven times. This symbolises being in a hurry to respond to Allah and show love for Allah, a compulsory part of the Hajj. The night of the tenth is spent back at **Mina**.

On the afternoon of the eleventh and again on the following day the pilgrims must again throw seven pebbles at each of the three jamarat or stone pillars in Mina.

Pilgrims must leave Mina for Makkah before sunset on the twelfth. If they are unable to leave Mina before sunset, they must perform the stoning ritual again on the thirteenth before returning to Makkah.

Finally, before leaving Makkah, pilgrims perform a farewell tawaf called the Tawaf al-Wada. They will begin to reflect on what the Hajj means for them personally. They will also show that they have completed the pilgrimage by an outward symbol, for example, many men will have their heads shaved, and women pilgrims will have 2.5 cm cut off their hair as a mark of their devotion.

Although it is not required as part of the Hajj, many pilgrims also travel to al-Madinah and the Mosque of the Prophet, where the prophet was buried in 632 CE. It was al-Madinah that first accepted the message of the Prophet when he left Makkah. The Hijrah was so important that it marks the beginning of the Islamic calendar.

The lessons learnt on Hajj

The Hajj is not only a physical journey to places connected to the Muslim faith but it is also about the importance of an inner journey. Islam means 'submission and peace in the will of Allah', so the outcome of the journey for the pilgrim should be a willingness to follow the way of Allah and share Allah's peace with all people.

The Hajj should be a time for spiritual growth and reflection. It should remind Muslims of the blessings of Allah and the prophets, Allah's messengers. It should encourage Muslims to think about their own level of devotion. To have seen the places where great things are believed to have happened can also reinforce their faith.

During the Hajj, there is time to think, to pray and to reflect on the meaning of Islam. By wearing **ihram**, the pilgrim has taken time to think about the mightiness of Allah compared with their own smallness.

Meeting with other believers from across the world can also have a powerful effect as it helps Muslims to realise that they are part of the worldwide community of Islam, the **ummah**. It is believed that going on Hajj enables Muslims to be more open to and tolerant of people from other religions, promoting peace and increasing belief in equality.

AO1 skills **ACTIVITIES**

Read the quotation below from the American, black Muslim leader, Malcolm X about his experiences on the Hajj. Why do you think going on the Hajj helped Malcolm X to overcome his racism against white people? What do you think people can do to overcome prejudice against other people, including Islamaphobia?

'I have been blessed to visit the Holy City of Makkah ... There were tens of thousands of pilgrims from all over the world. They were of all colors, from blue-eyed blondes to black-skinned Africans. But we were all participating in the same ritual, displaying a spirit of unity and brotherhood that my experiences in America had led me to believe never could exist between the white and the non-white.'

AO2 skills **ACTIVITIES**

Are submission and humility good qualities for 21st-century people to have? Give reasons for your answer, showing that you have thought about it from more than one point of view, making sure that you include Muslim opinions.

Create a PowerPoint presentation to show the most important parts of the Hajj and their meaning.

'Life is like a pilgrimage.' How might the Hajj mirror the internal spiritual journeys that Muslims make in their lives?

Why do Muslims celebrate Id-ul-Adha?

Id-ul-Adha

In the Islamic year, there are two Id celebrations. *Id* is an Arabic word meaning 'festival'. Id-ul-Adha is more serious than Id-ul-Fitr. Another name for Id-ul-Adha is 'The Day of Sacrifice' because Muslims remember **Ibrahim**'s willingness to sacrifice his son for Allah (see Topic 2.3).

The next two pages will help you to:

- identify and explain the important parts of Id-ul-Adha
- examine how Id-ul-Adha reflects Muslim beliefs about sacrifice and the role of Ibrahim in Islam
- evaluate how the festival shows the importance of following the will of Allah.

Id-ul-Adha prayers.

Allah commended Ibrahim for the faith he had shown in being willing to sacrifice his son, and declared that Muslim worship would no longer require human sacrifice. Ibrahim's example should inspire all Muslims to be faithful to Allah and to act as Ibrahim did. As Ibrahim was prepared to keep his promise to Allah despite the possible cost, Allah rewarded him and his people.

The sacrifice

The festival of Id-ul-Adha actually begins on 10 Dhul-Hijjah (the month of the **Hajj**). One of the most important acts of this festival is the sacrifice of an animal.

AO1 skills **ACTIVITIES**

Is it always right to keep your promises? Could it ever be right to break a promise? Give an example and a reason why that might be the case. Talk about these questions in a group of four and then one person has to report back to the class.

Every family has to make the decision to find an animal which they consider perfect. This could be a sheep, a goat, cow or even a camel. In many countries, the father of a family will slaughter the animal himself. In the UK, this is not allowed so the animal is killed in a special abattoir following halal rules. This means that when animals are slaughtered:

- the animal must not be frightened at the time the slaughter is about to happen
- the animal must be turned to face the holy city of **Makkah**, as the slaughterer prays and recalls the name of Allah
- the knife used must be very sharp so that when the jugular vein of the animal is cut, death follows very quickly
- it is important that all blood is drained from the animal as Muslims believe that any animal with blood still in the meat that is eaten will be unclean and not fit to eat.

If these rules are followed, the meat will then be considered to be halal.

After the animal is killed, the family that has had it slaughtered will have the right to keep one-third of it for their celebration for the festival. The remaining two-thirds are given either to their relatives or to the poor or those in need.

Surah 37:100–109

'O my Lord! Grant me a righteous (son)!'
So We gave him the good news of a boy ready to suffer and forbear.
Then, when (the son) reached (the age of) (serious) work with him, he said:
'O my son! I see in vision that I offer thee in sacrifice: Now see what is thy view!'
(The son) said: 'O my father! Do as thou art commanded: thou will find me, if Allah so wills one practising Patience and Constancy!'
So when they had both submitted their wills (to Allah), and he had laid him prostrate on his forehead (for sacrifice),
We called out to him 'O Abraham!'
'Thou hast already fulfilled the vision!' – thus indeed do We reward those who do right.
For this was obviously a trial –
And We ransomed him with a momentous sacrifice:
And We left (this blessing) for him among generations (to come) in later times:
'Peace and salutation to Abraham!'

REMEMBER THIS

Re-read the story of Ibrahim and Isma'il in Topic 2.3.

 FOR DEBATE

Are animal sacrifices appropriate in the 21st century? What do you think and why?

The quotation on the left about Ibrahim and Isma'il is from the Qur'an.

 **ACTIVITIES**

AO1 skills

Design a guide to explain Id-ul-Adha to a Year 7 student.

Read the story of Ibrahim and Isma'il in the Qur'an and then read Genesis 22:1–13. What is similar about the two? What is different?

Why do Muslims celebrate Id-ul-Fitr?

The next two pages will help you to:

- identify and explain the important parts of Id-ul-Fitr
- examine how Id-ul-Fitr reflects Muslim belief.

Muslims meeting for a celebration of Id-ul-Fitr in the UK.

Id-ul-Fitr

Id-ul-Fitr is a Muslim festival that marks the end of **Ramadan** and the formal end of the fast. *Fitr* means 'to break a fast'. Id-ul-Fitr is usually celebrated over three days and is called the 'Lesser Id' compared with the four days devoted to the more important Id-ul-Adha.

People will use Arabic greetings such as *Īd Mubarak* ('Blessed Id') or *'Īd sa' īd* ('Happy Id'). Some Muslim countries have developed their own customs and ways to acknowledge the festival.

On the first day of the festival, many Muslims will wake up early in the morning and have a small breakfast. Some may have stayed up all of the night before, to mark the end of the fasting time of Ramadan. Fasting will have been difficult for many, but there are important benefits. They believe that Allah will reward people for their devotion.

AO1 skills **ACTIVITIES**

What is the best gift that you have ever received? What is the worst gift you have ever received? What is the best gift you have ever given and why? Why do you think we give and receive gifts? Discuss these questions with the class.

People are encouraged to dress in their best clothes (new, if possible) and to attend a special Id prayer that is said in open areas like fields and squares as well as with other Muslims in the mosque.

On their way to the Id prayer, Muslims recite this *takbir* (proclamation of the greatness of Allah):

> God is the Greatest, God is the Greatest, God is the Greatest,
> There is no deity but God
> God is the Greatest, God is the Greatest
> and to God goes all praise

Before the Id prayer begins, every Muslim who is able must pay *zakat-ul-fitr* (or *sadaqat-ul-fitr*), a welfare payment for the month of Ramadan. This is about 2 kg of food (for example, wheat, barley, dates or raisins). People may choose to give the cash equivalent of what they would have spent on food.

Many Muslims give this money at the mosque where they worship. The imams (leaders of the mosque) then make sure that this is distributed to needy local Muslims before the start of the Id prayer. It can be given at any time during Ramadan and is often given early, so the person who receives the gift can use it for buying what they need to have a good Id celebration.

After the Id prayer is said at the mosque the iman gives the *khutbah* (sermon or talk). A *du'a* (prayer) is said at this point, asking for forgiveness, mercy and help for the plight of Muslims around the world. The khutbah reminds Muslims why the celebrations of Id, and features such as zaqat-ul-fitr, are so important.

Many people embrace the people sitting near them as a sign to remind themselves and others that the whole Muslim community or **ummah** is devoting itself at this time to think about the sacrifices of **Ibrahim**. Many Muslims choose to visit families and friends at this time.

After the prayers, some people visit the graveyards of their departed loved ones to show their respect and their gratitude to them.

Some Muslims also remember the story of how the angel Jibril descended from heaven with white clothes for each of the Prophet Muhammad's ﷺ grandsons, so they may well give each other the gift of new clothes to mark this festival.

RESEARCH NOTE

Use the Internet to find out how different countries celebrate Id-ul-Fitr.

AO1 skills ACTIVITIES

Id-ul-Fitr celebrates the appearance of the angel Jibril to the Prophet Muhammad ﷺ. Why is this so important to Muslims?

Compare the festivals of Id-ul-Adha and Id-ul-Fitr, explaining features of both celebrations and their significance to Muslims.

Why do Muslims celebrate Mawlid an-Nabi?

The next two pages will help you to:

- identify and explain the important parts of Mawlid an-Nabi
- understand why the celebration of the Prophet Muhammad's ﷺ birthday is important to some Muslims and why others do not celebrate it
- evaluate the importance of the festival to Muslims.

Muslims celebrate the birth of the Prophet Muhammad ﷺ.

Mawlid an-Nabi

Mawlid an-Nabi means the 'birth of the Prophet Muhammad ﷺ'. It takes place on the 12th day of the 3rd month in the Islamic year (Rabi-ul-Awwal). The birth of the prophet was first celebrated in Egypt in the 11th century CE, although some Muslim scholars believe that it has its roots in customs from the 8th century CE.

The word Mawlid is also used in some parts of the world for the birthday celebrations of other important Islamic leaders. Many of these are marked as public holidays in some Muslim countries.

AO1 skills ACTIVITIES

Work with a partner and think about what you need to do to plan a party for someone about to celebrate their 18th birthday. Present your ideas as a spider diagram.

Differences of view

Many Muslims, despite having high regard for Muhammad ﷺ, do not hold celebrations on this day. They believe that celebrating his birthday is inappropriate and not what the Prophet himself would have wanted. They follow Muhammad's ﷺ own followers who did not celebrate his birthday.

Some believe that they should observe the importance of the Prophet by fasting sometimes on a Monday when, according to tradition, Muhammad ﷺ was born. Other Muslims, however, do not believe that it should be celebrated because they do not see any clear references to doing so in the **Qur'an** or in the **Hadith**, which they say are the ultimate authorities for what should be done. They regard the Prophet's life as an example of self-control and obedience to the will of Allah, which they feel does not fit with a day celebrating the man Muhammad ﷺ.

Celebrating Mawlid

Mawlid is often celebrated with a large street procession and a carnival atmosphere. People spend time making sure that homes or mosques are decorated. Charity and food is distributed to the poor and needy. It is a very happy occasion, where families and friends spend time together, eat good food and spend money they have saved on sweets, toys, clothes or something else.

Many Muslims tell stories about the life of Muhammad ﷺ and encourage children to take part in poetic readings on this theme.

Celebrations around the world

Mawlid is celebrated in many Muslim countries and in other countries where Muslims have a presence, such as India, UK and Canada.

Some non-Muslim countries such as India have many Mawlid celebrations. What is believed to be a hair of Muhammad ﷺ is displayed after the morning prayers at Hazratbal shrine, on the outskirts of Srinagar, where thousands of people gather to take part in the night-long prayers to mark the event.

During Pakistan's Mawlid celebrations, the national flag is flown on all public buildings. A 31-gun salute is fired in Lahore, to mark the beginning of the celebration at first light. Cinemas show religious films on 11–12 Rabi-ul-Awwal, to help people reflect on the importance of the day.

RESEARCH NOTE

Find out about Mawlid an-Nabi in one Islamic country and present your findings as a labelled poster or a PowerPoint presentation.

AO2 skills **ACTIVITIES**

'Muhammad ﷺ would not have approved of a celebration of his birthday, as he would think this distracted from the message of Allah.' What might a Muslim response be to this? What do you think? Show that you have thought about it from more than one point of view and make sure that your answer refers to Muslim teachings.

Some Muslim scholars think that it is appropriate to have a fast day to mark Muhammad's ﷺ birthday. Do you agree with them? Give reasons for your answers, showing that you have thought about it from more than one point of view.

Graded examples for this topic

AO1

AO1 questions test what you know and how well you can explain and analyse things. Let's look at an AO1 question to see what examiners expect you to do.

Question

How do you think Muslims can benefit from going on the Hajj? [6 marks]

Student's answer

A Muslim can benefit from going on the Hajj as they can visit the places that are mentioned in their religion as important and they can get a sense of the things that Muhammad (PBUH) must have experienced.

Examiner's comment

This answer is a start at answering the question, but the description is very weak. The explanation only refers to some of the emotions a Muslim might have when they go on Hajj, not to the meaning and importance for Islam of the places they might visit. There is no real explanation given, so this would only receive the minimum marks. (*Level 1*)

Student's answer

A Muslim can benefit from the Hajj as it will help them to develop their understanding of the places that were important to their faith and will reinforce their understanding of what it means to be part of the ummah, the worldwide community of Muslims. It will also enable them to reflect with humility to God's call to them personally and through his servants Ibrahim and Muhammad (PBUH).

Examiner's comment

The answer gives a slightly better account of the experience of Hajj. However, it is still vague as it needs to use more examples. In particular it needs to explain how Muslims might feel when they go to particular places. This is a reasonable response at *Level 2* but needs more development.

Student's improved answer

A Muslim can benefit from the Hajj as it will help them to develop their understanding of the places that are important to their faith and will reinforce their understanding of what it means to be part of the ummah, the worldwide community of Muslims. Hajj will also enable a Muslim to reflect with humility to Allah's call to them personally and through his servants Ibrahim and Muhammad (PBUH). It is particularly important for Muslims to stone the pillars at Mina to show their rejection of Shaytan and also to stand at Arafat where they can remember the Prophet. Because there are so many Muslims on Hajj, all doing the same thing, they feel the strength of the ummah which will help them and strengthen their faith in submitting to Allah's will.

Examiner's comment

This is an excellent answer which clearly explains the importance of Hajj and how it might benefit a Muslim. (*Level 3*)

AO2

AO2 questions are about examining points of view and expressing your own views, using evidence and argument to support them. AO2 questions are worth 12 marks.

Examiners will use levels of response to judge the quality of your work and the best responses will have plenty of evidence to support different points of view. For AO2 there are four levels of response and for the top level the response will have a personal view supported by evidence and argument.

Question

'Life is like a pilgrimage.' Discuss this statement. You should include different, supported points of view and a personal viewpoint. You must refer to Islam in your answer. **[12 marks]**

Student's answer

When people say that life is like a pilgrimage they mean that each stage in your life moves you a bit further forward just as though you were going on a journey somewhere. However, Muslims might say that going on pilgrimage, Hajj, is very different because it is a duty to Allah as one of the Five Pillars and that because all the people there share the same experiences it is quite different from the pattern of someone's life.

Examiner's comment

This answer gives a clear explanation of a possible Muslim view. However, it only gives one view and a personal opinion and so can only reach the top of *Level 2*.

Student's improved answer

I believe that when people say that life is like a pilgrimage they mean that each stage in your life moves you a bit further forward just as though you were going on a journey somewhere. However, Muslims might say that going on pilgrimage, Hajj, is very different because it is a duty to Allah as one of the Five Pillars and that because all the people there share the same experiences it is quite different from the pattern of someone's life. On the other hand a Muslim might say that just as Hajj helps them to understand their religion more and to pass through the places where some of the Prophets were is, in some ways, like their journey through life where, as they grow older and learn more about Islam and Allah, it is a pilgrimage towards God.

Examiner's comment

This is a very good answer. It gives clear explanations of two possible Muslim views as well as a personal opinion. This reaches *Level 4*.

These specimen answers provide an outline of how you could construct your response. Space does not allow us to give a full response. The examiner will be looking for more detail in your actual exam responses.

Remember and Reflect

AO1 Describe, explain and analyse, using knowledge and understanding

Find the answer on:

1 Explain, in one sentence, what each of the following words means:
   a   Salat-ul-Jumu'ah
   b   wudu
   c   al-ummah
   d   Hajj.

PAGE 34, 35, 40

2 Why is the Hajj important to Muslims?

PAGE 41–42

3 Explain what Muslims understand by prayer.

PAGE 34–35

4 Why do some Muslims believe it is important to celebrate the Prophet Muhammad's birthday? Why do others think it is wrong to celebrate it?

PAGE 52–53

5 Explain, giving examples, the way Id-ul-Fitr is celebrated.

PAGE 50–51

6 Explain, giving examples, the different ways Id-ul-Adha is celebrated.

PAGE 48–49

7 Explain, in one sentence, what each of the following terms means:
   a   Hajj
   b   ihram
   c   the Ka'bah
   d   tawaf
   e   the plain of Arafat
   f   rami al-jamarat.

PAGE 40–45

8 Outline three ways in which Muslims might believe they benefit from the Hajj.

PAGE 47

9 Outline three ways in which Muslims believe they benefit from celebrating the festivals of Id-ul-Adha and Id-ul-Fitr.

PAGE 47–50

10 Explain the significance of Salat-ul-Jumu'ah to Muslims.

PAGE 34–35

11 Why do Muslims fast during Ramadan, and what does fasting involve?

PAGE 36–37

12 Explain the significance of the story of Ibrahim and Isma'il.

PAGE 38–39

13 Summarise the parts of the Hajj, explaining their significance to Muslims.

PAGE 40–41

AO2 Use evidence and reasoned argument to express and evaluate personal responses, informed insights, and differing viewpoints

1 Answer the following, giving as much detail as possible. You should give at least three reasons to support your response and also show that you have taken into account opposite opinions.
   a *Muslims need to go on Hajj to be true Muslims.*
   b *Do you think a Muslim can go on Hajj and not benefit from it?*
   c *Do you believe the pilgrimage to Makkah is helpful? Why or why not? Compare your response with that of a young Muslim who has not been to Makkah, an older Muslim who has and someone who does not believe in a God.*
   d *What would you say are the essential things a Muslim must do for the Hajj to be a truly spiritual event? Why?*

2 'The Hajj is just one journey amongst many. A person open to learning can learn about their relationship with God in any place.' How would a Muslim answer this? What do you think? Give reasons for your answers.

3 Why are festivals so important? Do you have a day which is important to you? What opportunities and challenges might Muslims have that arise from the festivals they celebrate? Include examples of Islamic festivals in your answer.

4 'The God represented in the story of Ibrahim and Isma'il is a bully.' What do you think? Give reasons for your answers, making sure that you have thought through the Islamic understandings of the story.

5 Copy out the table. As well as entering Key points add any other notes you think relevant, and give your personal response with reasons.

Special event or place	Key points	What I think and why
Salat-ul-Jumu'ah		
Hajj		
tawaf		
rami al-jamarat		
Id-ul-Adha		
Id-ul-Fitr		
Mawlid an-Nabi		

Topic 3: Major divisions and interpretations

The Big Picture

In this topic you will learn about the major divisions and interpretations of Islam by studying:

- the similarities and differences between Sunni, Shi'ah and Sufi Muslims
- how Islam is practised in the UK and in other parts of the world.

What?

You will:

- understand the reasons for the split between Sunni and Shi'ah
- explain how this split affects the beliefs and practices of Islam today
- learn the similarities and differences in Islamic belief and practice in the UK and other parts of the Muslim world and understand the reasons for these.

How?

By:

- selecting and recalling key information about the reasons behind the major divisions in Islam and Islam's practice in the UK and other parts of the world
- thinking about the importance of these divisions for Muslims today
- evaluating your own beliefs about the divisions and practices of Islam in the UK and other parts of the world.

Why?

Because:

- these divisions are reflected in many aspects of Muslim belief and practice such as festivals, worship and sources of authority
- understanding the divisions in Islam can help you to appreciate why different Muslims think and act in the way that they do.

Islam is a religion of peace. Throughout history the teachings of many religions have been misinterpreted by extremists.

GET STARTED

Imagine you are with supporters of different football teams, for example, Manchester United, Celtic, Real Madrid and AC Milan.

1   What unites the supporters of these teams?

2   What is different about the supporters of these teams?

3   How might you expect football to be played and supported in different countries around the world?

4   Do you feel that differences are a good thing or a bad thing? Should we all be the same?

Major divisions and interpretations

KEY INFORMATION

- Islam is divided into two main groupings called Sunni and Shi'ah.
- The Sunnis and Shi'ahs split over who should be the successor or khalifah to the Prophet Muhammad ﷺ.
- The Sunnis believed Muhammad's ﷺ successor should be an individual chosen by the community, and Abu Bakr, the prophet's close friend, was chosen.
- The Shi'ahs believed Muhammad's ﷺ successor should be a member of the Prophet's family, and they followed his cousin Ali.
- A war was fought between the Sunnis and Shi'ahs on the plain of Karbala, on which Ali's son, Hussein, was martyred and he has become a central figure in Shi'ah belief.
- Although both Sunnis and Shi'ahs describe themselves as Muslim, they practise their religion in different ways.
- The Muslim world is divided into five law schools which have the power to interpret the scriptures on how Islam should be practised.
- These law schools dominate in certain regions of the world.
- As Muslim communities have left their regions to make a new life elsewhere they have taken their beliefs and practices with them. This is why, for example, the treatment of Muslim women varies around the world.
- In the UK today there is a Muslim community made up of people from around the Muslim world.
- There are also strong cultural influences within Islam, for example, Muslims from Africa have a different view of Islam from Muslims who have originated from the Middle East or Pakistan.

KEY QUESTIONS

KNOWLEDGE AND UNDERSTANDING

- What is the major division in the Muslim world?
- Why did the major split occur in the Muslim world so soon after the death of the Prophet?
- What are some of the key differences in belief and practice between Sunnis and Shi'ahs?
- Why can the British Muslim community be described as divided?
- What differences might a British Muslim notice in the way that Islam is practised in other parts of the world?

ANALYSIS AND EVALUATION

- How important is the martyrdom of Hussein in Shi'ah Islam?
- Is Islam a united or a divided religion?
- 'Islam in the UK can never really speak with one voice.' How far is this true? Consider your own views.
- 'Shi'ahs and Sunnis have more in common than they have differences.' How far is this true?

Abu Bakr Muhammad's ﷺ close friend and father-in-law; who succeeded Muhammad ﷺ when he died.

Ali Muhammad's ﷺ cousin and son-in-law; Shi'ahs believe he should have succeeded Muhammad ﷺ when he died.

Ashura A major Shi'ah festival which commemorates the martyrdom of Hussein.

Hidden Imam Whether there were five, seven or twelve special Imams, the last mysteriously disappeared and is still believed to be alive, able to guide the current Shi'ah leaders. It is believed that the Hidden Imam will reappear on the Day of Judgement.

Hussein The grandson of Muhammad ﷺ and Shi'ah leader who died a martyr on the plain of Karbala; Shi'ahs believe he should have been the Muhammad's ﷺ successor.

imam A person who leads communal prayer, administers ceremonies and offers their communities spiritual guidance.

Imams The Imams are twelve individuals who were the direct descendents of Ali. The Imams are regarded as divinely chosen religious figures who act as intermediaries between Allah and the rest of the community. They are considered to be free from sin and infallible.

Karbala The place in modern Iraq where the Shi'ah leader Hussein was martyred. A major centre of Shi'ah pilgrimage today.

khalifah Steward or custodian (of the earth).

martyr A person who dies for a belief or cause.

Muáwiya The fifth khalifah, cousin of the murdered Uthman, and father of Yazid.

Shi'ah A Muslim who believes Ali should have succeeded Muhammad ﷺ, because he was Muhammad's ﷺ cousin. They form about 11 per cent of the total Muslim population.

Sufi A group within Islam, concerned with mystical experience and with developing their relationship with Allah. Sufis can be Sunni or Shi'ah.

Sunni A Muslim who believes Abu Bakr should have succeeded Muhammad ﷺ. They follow the Sunnah or the way of Muhammad ﷺ. Sunni Muslims form about 89 per cent of the Muslim population worldwide.

Uthman The khalifah or successor to Muhammad ﷺ who organised the official version of the Qur'an.

Yazid The opponent of Hussein at Karbala, and son of Muáwiya.

FOR INTEREST The war in present-day Iraq has been described as a civil war between the Sunni majority and the Shi'ah minority. It is a war rooted in nearly 1400 years of conflict in the Muslim world.

Do you think it is easier or harder to end a war that has gone on for hundreds of years than a recent war? Perhaps it is so old that people are tired of it and want to start afresh. Perhaps others want to keep it going because of family and friends who have died fighting for their cause. What do you think?

The divided world of Islam

A divided Muslim world

When the word 'Islam' is used it gives the impression that all Muslims are the same, and that they worship and practise their faith in exactly the same way. However, the word 'Muslim' simply means to 'submit to the will of Allah' and there are many different ways of doing this and interpreting how this can be done. In many ways, Islam is not a united religion; it is, in fact, divided into two main groups called the **Sunnis** and the **Shi'ahs**.

It is difficult to get precise figures on the worldwide Muslim population today. However, estimates suggest that there are more than 1 billion Muslims and that this figure is growing. Of this world population, Sunni Islam forms the majority and Shi'ah Islam is a significant but growing minority.

Islam is a worldwide religion and there are Muslim communities in virtually every country of the world. The majority of these communities are Sunni but there are Shi'ah communities concentrated in certain parts of the world. The map will help you identify the main concentrations of Islam in the world today.

The next two pages will help you to:

- explain that there are three main divisions in Islam: Sunni, Shi'ah and Sufi
- evaluate some of the differences between these groups.

AO1 skills ACTIVITIES

Name three Sunni Muslim countries.

Name the three countries which have a Shi'ah majority.

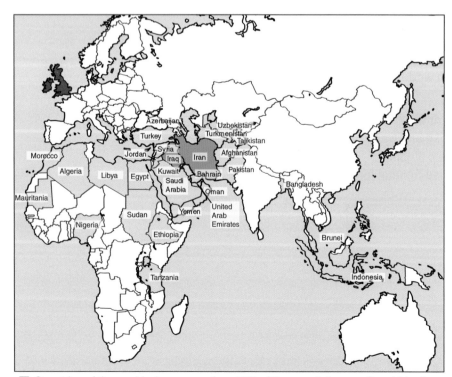

☐ Countries of the world where more than 50% of the population are Sunni Muslims
☐ Countries of the world where more than 50% of the population are Shi'a Muslims

Shi'ah Islam: religion of extremism?

Shi'ah Islam is in the minority in the Muslim world.

In the Lebanon, Hezbollah ('the Party of God') is a Shi'ah movement locked in a war with the state of Israel.

Parts of the city of Baghdad have been segregated into Sunni and Shi'ah zones.

Sufi Islam

As well as the two large groups of Muslims, Sunni and Shi'ah, there is a third group known as **Sufi** Islam. Sufi Muslims may be either Sunni or Shi'ah. There is no particular belief or practice which distinguishes Sufism from other Muslim groups.

The Sufi tradition is concerned with mystical experience and with the development of Muslims' relationship with Allah. Sufis are similar to Shi'ah Muslims and are opposed to people's concerns about wealth and worldliness.

In Arabic, Sufism is called *Tasawwuf* ('dressed in wool'). Sometimes Sufis are called *Fuqara* ('the poor').

Tawhid ('there is no God but Allah') is central to Sufi belief. This has been developed into the idea that there is nothing in existence except for Allah. Allah and creation are two parts of one thing – *wahdat al-wujud*.

The largest order of Sufis is the Naqshbandis. Their current leader, Shaykh Nazim Adil al-Haqqani, is the fortieth in his line of **khalifahs**, which traces its origins to **Abu Bakr**.

Sufism can be traced back to the time of **Muhammad** ﷺ but only became important in the early 10th century. By the end of that century it had spread through Iraq, Iran, Al Hijaz (western Saudi Arabia) and Egypt.

Sufism works to educate people and increase their spirituality. Sufis do missionary work throughout the world.

Many Sufi Muslims celebrate Mawlid an-Nabi, the Prophet's birthday. They also make visits to tombs such as those of *ziyara* (honoured Sufi shaykhs). They may pray to these figures asking for their intercession with Allah.

Some Sufis also listen to music and poetry as part of their worship. A particular feature of Sufi practice is *dhikr* (ritual repetition of phrases containing the name of Allah).

The origins of the Sunni/Shi'ah split

The Shi'ah Shrine of Ali at Najaf in modern Iraq.

The beginning of the Sunni/Shi'ah split

The **Sunni/Shi'ah** split was caused by disagreement over who should succeed the Prophet **Muhammad** ﷺ. Some people within the Muslim community felt the right and logical choice of **khalifah** (successor) should have been Muhammad's ﷺ cousin **Ali**: he was the first convert to Islam and was also Muhammad's ﷺ son-in-law (married to Muhammad's ﷺ youngest daughter and only surviving child, Fatima). Ali was also a leader in the Muslim army which had expanded Islam beyond the boundaries of Arabia. Muhammad ﷺ had suggested that Ali should be his successor.

In June 632 CE the Prophet Muhammad ﷺ died, probably of pneumonia, aged 63. The Muslim community met and ignored Ali's claims to the succession. Instead they chose Muhammad's ﷺ friend and father in-law, Abu Bakr, to be his successor. Abu Bakr had close

AO1 skills ACTIVITIES

Should leadership of an organisation pass down a family line or should the organisation's membership be able to elect their leader? What are the advantages and disadvantages of both systems?

connections to the Prophet and was also popular among the various tribes in Arabia at the time. It was claimed that the election of Abu Bakr took place when Ali was burying the Prophet and that he was not present at the meeting to declare his case. However, the supporters of Abu Bakr claimed that Muhammad ﷺ had supported his succession.

As a result of Ali's failure to be elected, and the perceived unfairness of this, his supporters formed themselves into the Party of Ali (Shiat Ali, now known as Shi'ah). They felt that the khalifah should be a member of Muhammad's ﷺ family line, represented by Ali. Those who did not support Ali became known as the Sunni, from the Arabic word *Sunnah*, which means 'custom or tradition'.

Abu Bakr died a natural death and was succeeded by two further khalifahs named Umar and **Uthman**, both of whom were murdered. The election of Uthman must have been particularly difficult for Ali since he belonged to a tribe which had fought long and hard against Muhammad ﷺ in the days when Muhammad ﷺ was trying to establish Islam. However, he was known as an extremely generous person and had married two of the daughters of the Prophet.

Ali chosen as the fourth khalifah

In 656 CE the third khalifah Uthman was murdered. Ali was the only individual who had enough support to become khalifah and he was duly elected. Even though he was elected, there were many in the Muslim world who objected to this and he had to fight against his opponents to establish his position.

As Islam grew and expanded, many of Ali's original supporters left their homes in Arabia and went to settle in new lands in what is now modern-day Iraq, so Ali's power base shifted from Arabia to Iraq. Ali had a new opponent, **Muáwiya**, the cousin of the murdered third khalifah Uthman, who felt that Ali had not brought his cousin's killers to justice. This led to a civil war in the Muslim world but this resulted in a draw with no clear winner. Matters came to a head in 661 CE when Ali was murdered. Muáwiya was the most powerful individual in the Muslim world, so he had himself declared the next khalifah.

Continued disagreement

However, the supporters of Ali were not happy with Muáwiya declaring himself the next khalifah. They chose Ali's eldest son, Hassan, who was also the Prophet Muhammad's ﷺ grandson, as khalifah instead. To avoid yet another civil war and further bloodshed, Muáwiya made an offer to the followers of Ali. The offer was that Muáwiya would continue to be khalifah but that when he died, Hassan would be elected to the position.

However, Hassan died before Muáwiya (some argued that he was murdered). Muáwiya then used this death as an excuse to arrange for his own son **Yazid** to be elected as the next khalifah. The Shi'ahs responded by declaring Ali's youngest son **Hussein** (a grandson of Muhammad ﷺ) as the next khalifah. This set the scene for one of the most important and dramatic events in Shi'ah history and belief.

ACTIVITIES

'Divisions within a religion are always a bad thing.' Do you agree with this statement? Give reasons to support your answer and consider how a Muslim might respond.

The plain of Karbala

The next two pages will help you to:

- explain what happened on the plain of Karbala
- consider the importance of the martyrdom of Hussein.

The headless body of Imam Hussein was left on the plain of Karbala.

Hussein versus Yazid

When the **khalifah Muáwiya** declared that he would not accept any more of **Ali's** descendants as successors, war broke out again in the Muslim world. Ali's youngest son **Hussein** declared himself to be the next khalifah and attempted to raise an army in what is now Iraq. However, Hussein's attempt to raise soldiers met with little enthusiasm and he soon found himself with only 70 supporters, cornered by **Yazid** on the plain of **Karbala**. Yazid had an army of several thousand. The date was 10 October 680 CE.

Hussein and his small band of supporters suffered greatly. They were surrounded on a barren desert plain without any water, even though the River Euphrates was only a short distance away. For eight days they endured terrible thirst while negotiations went on between Hussein and Yazid. Not only was Hussein trapped but so were his wife, sister and young son.

The martyrdom of Hussein

Negotiations between the leaders were not progressing. Hussein rode towards Yazid's army on a white horse holding his baby son, Abdullah, in his arms. As he neared Yazid's army, Hussein held up the baby, who was the great grandson of **Muhammad** ﷺ, declaring the child to be innocent and demanding that water be given to him. Yazid's soldiers responded by firing arrows, one of which went through the baby's neck and pinned him to Hussein's arm. Hussein returned to his wife and handed the wounded child over to her (the baby died and was succeeded by his brother Ali Zayn 'l-'Abidin, who later became a Shi'ah leader).

With his few remaining men, Hussein led a suicidal attack against the overwhelming numbers of his opponents as a witness to justice. Hussein and his men were wiped out in a storm of arrows. He was decapitated and his head was put on public display but was later returned for burial.

Karbala – a place of Shi'ah pilgrimage

Hussein was buried at Karbala. For Shi'ah Muslims Karbala has become a place of tremendous significance and pilgrimage, almost rivalling Makkah and al-Madinah. Shi'ah Muslims regard Hussein as a **martyr**. His martyrdom on the plain of Karbala has become a central belief for modern Shi'ahs and is remembered during the festival of **Ashura**.

AO1 skills ACTIVITIES

What is a martyr?

Can you think of any examples of martyrs?

AO2 skills ACTIVITIES

Why could Hussein be described as a martyr for the Shi'ahs?

'There is never a belief or cause worth dying for.' What is your view on this? What might Muslims say about it?

Muslims arriving at Karbala for the festival of Ashura.

The festival of Ashura

The next two pages will help you to:

- explain what happens at the festival of Ashura
- consider why Sunni and Shi'ah Muslims might mark this festival differently.

The Shrine of Hussein at Karbala in Iraq.

Background

Hussein became a martyr for the Shi'ah cause and his martyrdom is remembered in the festival of **Ashura**.

The origins of Ashura go back to the early years of **Muhammad** ﷺ. At that time there was a close connection between Islam and Judaism (Jews and Christians were known as 'People of the Book'). According to some Muslim traditions, Muhammad ﷺ requested Muslims to fast with Jews on the Jewish Day of Atonement (Yom Kippur). As Islam developed and the calendar changed, Ashura was replaced by the month of Ramadan which took on some of its characteristics. **Sunni** Muslims who celebrate Ashura have a recommended fast on this day, but it is really Shi'ah Muslims for whom the festival is particularly important.

ACTIVITIES

What does the Shi'ah festival of Ashura remember?

Why does fasting and physical suffering play such an important part in the festival?

The central focus of the festival is the Iraqi city of **Karbala** which contains the shrine of Hussein. Shi'ahs have only recently been allowed to resume the festival here because Saddam Hussein the President of Iraq from 1979–2003 had previously forbidden the celebration. The festival takes place during the Muslim month of Muharram, the first month of the year, and lasts for ten days. Although the focus is on Karbala, it is celebrated by all Shi'ah communities around the world.

What happens at Ashura?

Celebration of Ashura is a central feature of Shi'ah Islam. Some of the main features are:

- Passion plays, which remind Shi'ahs of the martyrdom of Hussein. In Iran, which is a Shi'ah country, a criminal is often released from prison on condition that he agrees to play the role of the villain **Yazid**.

- The offering of prayers for Hussein, to reinforce the Shi'ah belief of being able to get to paradise by faith in atoning (making amends for sin).

- A period of fasting. The concept of self-denial, as shown through fasting, is very strong in Islam and serves two purposes during the festival:
  - it is a reminder of the suffering which Hussein and his followers experienced at Karbala
  - it develops a sense of self-discipline and denial. The whole community endures hunger and thirst. This allows greater empathy with the poor and could lead to greater generosity.

Suffering and martyrdom are graphically displayed during the festival. There is much weeping and many acts of self-mutilation (such as hitting oneself with a chain). The shedding of blood is more graphic because people often wear white clothing.

ACTIVITIES

Why should an event that occurred nearly 1400 years ago be such an important part of Shi'ah Islam today?

How far would you be prepared to go for something which you strongly believe in?

During Ashura some Shi'ah Muslims whip themselves with chains while they remember the death of Hussein.

Topic 3: Major divisions and interpretations 69

The differences between Sunnis and Shi'ahs

The next two pages will help you to:

- understand and explain the differences between Sunni and Shi'ah Muslims
- consider the importance of these differences.

FOR DEBATE

Can you tell the difference between a Sunni woman and a Shi'ah woman just by their appearance?

Shi'ah women.

Sunni women.

What are they key differences between Sunni and Shi'ah beliefs and practices?

The **Sunni/Shi'ah** split has led to some differences in the way they practise Islam and to some different beliefs. The main differences are listed below.

- Shi'ahs believe that **Ali** was the rightful heir of **Muhammad** , and that the power which Ali was given was passed on through his family line.
- Shi'ahs believe that special, divinely chosen figures called **Imams** have appeared. They do not sin and act as intermediaries (go-betweens) between Allah and the human race.

REMEMBER THIS

Refer back to Topics 1.2 and 1.4 to remember why Muhammad is called the 'Seal of the Prophets'.

- The chosen Imams have the power to interpret the Qur'an.
- Shi'ahs are waiting for a final **Hidden Imam** (the Mahdi), who is in the background guiding the Shi'ahs but who will come forward before the Day of Judgement.
- Shi'ahs regard the first three **khalifahs** – **Abu Bakr**, Umar and **Uthman** – as false leaders.
- Shi'ahs celebrate extra festivals, the most important of which is **Ashura**.
- Shi'ah fasting during the month of Ramadan ends only after the sun has completely set. During Ramadan, Shi'ahs remember the death of Ali on three special days of mourning.
- Recalling the death of **Hussein** will save Shi'ahs from their sins on the Day of Judgement and therefore they will gain their place in heaven.
- When performing Salah (one of the Five Pillars of Islam), a Shi'ah should prostrate their head on some earth or a block of dried mud from the plain of **Karbala**. This is in remembrance of Hussein's death as a martyr.
- Shi'ahs also make extra pilgrimages to the shrine of Hussein in Karbala and the shrine of Ali at Najaf in Iraq.
- Saints and miracles play a powerful part in Shi'ah belief and practice. Muhammad's ﷺ daughter, Fatima, is a revered figure in Shi'ah Islam.
- Some Shi'ahs believe that the current form of the Qur'an is not final and can be added to by the Imams. They believe that the khalifah Uthman, in putting together the Qur'an, missed out reference to the power of the Imams.
- Shi'ahs include an extra phrase in the Shahadah (the most important of the Five Pillars of Islam): 'I bear witness that there is no god but Allah, that Muhammad is the messenger of Allah, *and that Ali is beloved of Allah.*'
- Shi'ah beliefs about additional Imams makes it difficult for them to accept that Muhammad ﷺ is Allah's final messenger or 'Seal of the Prophets'.
- In Sunni Islam, zakah (one of the Five Pillars of Islam) is sometimes paid to the state but in Shi'ah Islam it is paid to their religious leaders. Shi'ahs pay an additional 20 per cent tax on all profits and this goes to their leaders.
- Shi'ahs are allowed to have a temporary marriage called a *muta*. This marriage can be set for an agreed amount of time.
- In Shi'ah countries such as Iran, Shi'ah **imams** have considerable power and can make changes in the law without the need for a democratic process.

 **ACTIVITIES**

Copy and complete the table below to show the differences between Sunni and Shi'ah beliefs and practices.

Shi'ah	Sunni

Give examples of two beliefs and two practices which are different between Shi'ah and Sunni Islam.

 **ACTIVITIES**

'The differences between Sunni and Shi'ah Muslims are so great that it is impossible not to see Islam as two separate religions.' What is your view and the views of others on this? What do you think Sunni and Shi'ah Muslims would say?

The similarities between Sunnis and Shi'ahs

The next two pages will help you to:

- understand and explain the similarities between Sunni and Shi'ah Muslims
- consider the importance of these similarities.

The shrine of Fatima al-Ma'sumah in Qom, Iran.

Similarities between Sunni and Shi'ah Muslims

Although there are some major differences between **Sunnis** and **Shi'ahs**, both regard themselves as true Muslims or 'one who has submitted to the will of Allah'. Throughout the history of Islam, both groups have often lived and worshipped side by side. Some of the similarities are listed below.

- Both groups use the Qur'an or the revealed word of Allah as the basis of their beliefs and practices.
- Both groups acknowledge **Muhammad** ﷺ as the true messenger of Allah.

- They both use the Hadith and Sunnah as sources of authority.
- Sunnis and Shi'ahs both worship in the same type of religious building, a mosque.
- Both groups practise the Five Pillars of Islam:
  - The Shahadah is used by Shi'ahs as well as Sunnis, although Shi'ahs include an extra phrase.
  - Both groups practise sawm (fasting) during the month of Ramadan, although there are some minor differences in actual practices.
  - Both groups go on Hajj (pilgrimage) to the city of Makkah in Saudi Arabia.
  - Salah is performed five times a day facing towards Makkah.
  - Zakah is collected by both communities but there may be variations in the actual method of collection.
- Both groups use Arabic as the language of prayer, worship and the reading of the Qur'an.
- Sunnis and Shi'ahs believe in akhirah (afterlife) and the Day of Judgement.
- Shari'ah law operates in both communities and similar rules are observed regarding the eating of halal food, dress, modesty and sexual behaviour.
- Beliefs about angels and jinn (beings created by Allah from fire) are held in both communities.
- Both communities observe Salat-ul-Jumu'ah (Friday prayers).

Shi'ah shrines of Iran

Unusually for a Muslim country, Iran has 1100 shrines to remember various saints and **Imams**. An estimated 3 million pilgrims visit these various shrines annually. It is believed that the Twelve Imams of Shi'ah Islam can intercede for the living and the dead, that is, mediate on their behalf with Allah, on the matter of forgiveness of sins. As a result many cemeteries are built close to the shrines. It is also customary in Iran to leave donations of land or property to the shrines in order to generate income for them. This money can be used to run the shrines and also help the poor.

ACTIVITIES

Identify five ways in which Sunni and Shi'ah Muslims have similar beliefs and practices.

ACTIVITIES

In what ways could the major division in Islam be considered both positive and negative?

How might Muslims work to heal the division between Sunnis and Shi'ahs?

'Divisions in religion don't matter as long as everyone worships the same God.' Explain your own view and the views of others on this issue with reference to the Sunni/ Shi'ah split.

The development of Shi'ah Islam after Hussein

The next two pages will help you to:

- explain how Shi'ah Islam developed after the martyrdom of Hussein
- consider the role of the Hidden Imam in Shi'ah Islam.

The shrine of Imam Muhammed Taqi al-Jawad, the ninth Imam, in Karbala.

After the death of Hussein

The martyrdom of **Hussein** at **Karbala** did not end the Party of **Ali** but caused it to become a more secretive group. **Shi'ahs** were mainly based in what is now Iraq. In 750 CE they became strong enough to bring most of the Muslim world under their control. However, the Shi'ahs were in the minority, and so, to escape persecution, many Shi'ah communities began to move eastwards and settled in large numbers in Iran and Pakistan.

ACTIVITIES

Look at the picture of the Shi'ah Imam's shrine. Why is it important for Shi'ahs to visit such a site?

Can you think of any places and sites where you might go to remember something special or important?

Fivers, Seveners and Twelvers

Central to Shi'ah belief – and a fundamental difference with the **Sunnis** – is the idea of the power of the **Imams**. These are not the same as the imams found in Sunni Muslim communities who lead people in prayer, administer ceremonies and offer their communities spiritual guidance. Instead, the Imams are twelve individuals who were the direct descendents of Ali. They lived between 632 CE and 874 CE. The Imams are regarded as divinely chosen religious figures who act as intermediaries between Allah and the rest of the community. They are considered to be free from sin and they are also infallible (are never wrong). Each Imam was appointed by the previous Imam.

The life of each Imam is recorded in detail and each life showed unusual characteristics, including being born circumcised, speaking from the womb or immediately after birth, being able to perform miracles and having a deep mystical knowledge of Allah. Each Imam contributed to the development of Shi'ah Islam.

Shi'ahs are divided into three major groups called Fivers, Seveners and Twelvers. Each group is based on whether they believe in five, seven or twelve Imams. All three groups believe that the last Imam went into hiding and is known as the **Hidden Imam**. The Twelvers are in the majority in the Shi'ah world and are the dominant group in Iran.

The Hidden Imam

The Hidden Imam is a final Imam who mysteriously disappeared without dying and is still believed to be alive. Shi'ahs believe that the Hidden Imam is still present in the world although he is invisible. He appears to worshippers in prayers and dreams. The Hidden Imam is given the title of *Mahdi* ('Guided One') and it is believed that he will reappear at some point in the future to bring about the end of the world. Some Shi'ahs believe that the Hidden Imam will be the prophet Isa (Jesus).

ACTIVITIES

Explain the importance of the Imams to Shi'ahs.

What is meant by the terms 'Fivers', 'Seveners' and 'Twelvers'?

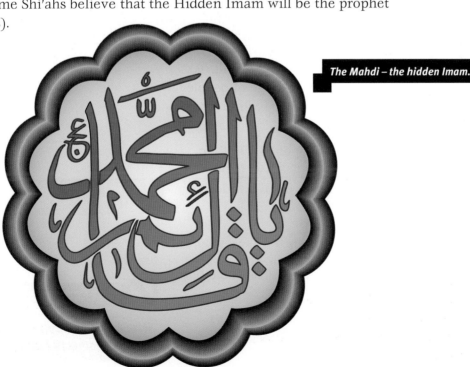

The Mahdi – the hidden Imam.

Modern Islam in the UK: a divided or united community?

The next two pages will help you to:

- understand the Muslim community in the UK
- consider the divisions between Muslims in the UK.

 **ACTIVITIES**

What do you think of when you hear or read the words 'British Muslims'?

East is East *was a very successful film which showed the problems faced by a Pakistani immigrant and his white non-Muslim wife in bringing up a family of British-born Muslim children in 1970s Salford.*

The diversity of the British Muslim community

If the words 'British Muslim' are mentioned, many people might automatically imagine a whole group of people, possibly of Pakistani origin, who all believe, act and worship in the same way. However, this picture does not reflect the British Muslim community at all. To use the term 'Muslim' in Britain is to describe a wide range of people who share many common ideas and beliefs but who have different ways of showing them.

The 2001 UK Census revealed a total UK population of 58.8 million people, of whom 1.6 million (or 2.7%) declared themselves to be Muslim. However, this Muslim community is made up of a wide range of different cultural and ethnic groups:

- 658,000 (42.5%) are of Pakistani origin
- 260,000 (16.0%) are of Bangladeshi origin
- 180,000 (11.6%) are white; of these 63,000 are white British and others are from elsewhere such as Eastern Europe
- 132,000 (8.5%) are of Indian origin
- 96,000 (6.2%) are Black African from countries such as Nigeria, Somalia and Kenya.

 **RESEARCH NOTE**

Research the requirements for Muslim women's clothing.

Cultural divisions

In the UK, there are large communities of Muslims from Malaysia, Egypt, Turkey, Iran, Iraq, Saudi Arabia, Cyprus and Indonesia. Each community has brought with it aspects of its own national identity and culture. These cultural differences affect many Islamic practices in Britain, for example, the design and use of mosques by different nationalities such as Turks, Pakistanis, Moroccans, Arabs and native-born reverts (people who have returned to a former belief). Different nationalities can also have different attitudes towards marriage, food and style of dress. Fifty per cent of all Muslims in the UK are British born and this adds a British perspective to the cultural mix.

Sunni/Shi'ah split in the UK

The worldwide **Sunni/Shi'ah** split also exists between British Muslims. There are major differences in beliefs and practices and there are many mosques which are attended only by Shi'ahs or by Sunnis.

The law schools and interpretation of Islam

Muslims live according to Shari'ah law, which is based on the teachings of the Qur'an and the life of **Muhammad** ﷺ. These laws are constantly changing as they keep pace with developments in the modern world. Five separate law schools developed during the 9th and 10th centuries CE to decide the nature of the Shari'ah law; four were Sunni schools and one was Shi'ah. Although each law school is based on the Qur'an, Hadith and Sunnah, they interpret these authorities differently. The different law schools dominate different areas of the Muslim world:

* Hanifite School: Turkey, Iraq, India and Pakistan
* Hanbalite School: Saudi Arabia
* Shafi'íte School: Egypt, Syria, Indonesia, Malaysia and East Africa
* Malikite School: North Africa and West Africa
* Jaafari School: which is Shi'ah.

The different law schools agree broadly on many issues but often disagree over small details. For example, they differ over how women should dress in public. Some law schools teach that a veil is required or that women should practise purdah (covering the whole body). Others take the view that a hijab (a simple headscarf) is sufficient, and there are various ways in which this can be worn along with modern Western-style clothes.

No single law school decides the standards for the whole British Muslim community. Instead, British Muslims tend to follow the law school which dominated their country of origin.

Modern British Muslim women.

ACTIVITIES

How large is the British Muslim community?

What are the main divisions of British Muslims?

ACTIVITIES

To what extent do divisions between British Muslims help or hinder the Muslim community?

What does the term 'British Muslim' mean to you now? (Look back at your answer to the first activity on the page opposite.)

Look at the picture of British Muslim women. What is your reaction to them? Do the differences in dress suggest a united or divided Muslim community in Britain today?

How is Islam practised in the UK?

The next two pages will help you to:

- understand how Islam is practised in the UK
- evaluate the challenges facing Muslims in the UK.

Challenges for Islam in the UK

Because Muslims make up only 2.7 per cent of the total UK population, there are many practical challenges for the practice of Islam in the UK. Not only does Islam have to deal with its own internal divisions, it also has to operate in a largely non-Muslim society which may sometimes be suspicious of it or even hostile towards it.

Since the major terrorist attack in New York in 2001 and the London bombings of 2005, and although the vast majority of Muslims have been shocked and outraged by these events, Islam in the UK has operated in an environment which can sometimes be suspicious and hostile.

How is Islam reported in the media?

The media often portrays Islam in a negative way.

The few people who support extreme actions have received wide media coverage. Such coverage has generated the stereotyped ideas that all Muslims are terrorists and fanatics.

How Islam affects everyday activities

The role of women

In traditional Muslim societies, men go to work and women tend the needs of the home. In many Muslim countries around the world this is still the case. However, in the UK, many Muslim women are gaining high levels of education and are then going into the world of employment and business. Such independence for women can sometimes cause conflict between their seeking a modern lifestyle and their parents and family if their family have more traditional attitudes.

There is also the issue of how Muslim women should dress in public. Many young Muslim women do not wear the hijab (headscarf). Others believe they should wear purdah (complete veil). Some young Muslim women are pressurised by their parents to wear the hijab, whereas others wear it against their parents' wishes.

ACTIVITIES AO1 skills

What are people's reactions to terrorist bombings?

Anti-Islamic protesters.

Money and finance

In British society the borrowing and lending of money at agreed rates of interest is an accepted way of life, whether it is borrowing a mortgage to buy a house, taking out a loan or running up a credit card debt or bank overdraft. However, the charging and paying of interest goes against the teachings of the Qur'an.

The world of work

There are certain jobs and careers in a non-Muslim society which Shari'ah law forbids Muslims from undertaking, such as jobs which involve the production and selling of alcohol, anything to do with gambling or the sex industry.

Muslims need to find sympathetic employers who will accommodate the requirements of the daily Salah or attending Salat-ul-Jumu'ah. Special consideration needs to be given to employees who are fasting during Ramadan or who need time off work to go on Hajj or celebrate Id-ul-Fitr or Id-ul-Adha.

Shari'ah Councils

In a wholly Muslim society, religion and the legal system are not separate frameworks but operate together. Shari'ah law, which is based on the principles of the Qur'an, is the legal system in some Muslim countries. Shari'ah law courts do not exist in the UK but there are Shari'ah Councils. British laws are created by the UK Parliament. In 2008, the Archbishop of Canterbury suggested introducing voluntary Shari'ah law courts to judge minor disputes and there was a hugely negative outcry from a mainly non-Muslim public.

Marriage and sex

Traditional Islamic practices such as arranged marriages and values such as sex only within marriage are under increasing pressure in the UK. The impact of the media and greater mixing with non-Muslims is influencing attitudes of many second-, third- and fourth-generation Muslims.

Madrassahs

Many mosques in the UK offer madrassahs (mosque schools) to enable Muslim parents to have their children educated in an Islamic way. Children attend the madrassah in addition to the ordinary schooling they receive. However, many madrassahs have been criticised because they are often run by **imams** who were born and educated abroad. They may have little or no cultural identity with the children they teach and their view of Islam has sometimes been questioned. Nevertheless, madrassahs give young people the opportunity to learn Arabic and understand more about their religion, as well as giving them greater opportunity to meet and mix with other members of the Muslim community.

AO1 skills ACTIVITIES

What kinds of problems might Muslims living in Britain experience in practising their faith?

AO2 skills ACTIVITIES

In a largely non-Muslim society, are Muslim women regarded as being free and equal, or are they perceived as downtrodden?

What could be done in British society to make it easier for a Muslim to practise their religion?

'It is impossible to live a Muslim way of life in a non-Muslim country.' What is your view on this? What do you think a Muslim might say?

How is Islam practised in other parts of the world?

Islam in the rest of the world

If a British Muslim were to travel to other parts of the Islamic world, they would be able to recognise many practices but they would also notice differences and variations.

Turkey

The population of Turkey is 97 per cent Muslim, the majority of whom are **Sunnis**. In 1923, the country was modernised by a revered Turkish leader, Mustafa Kemal Ataturk. He believed that traditional Islamic practices hindered Turkey's progress in the modern world. As a result, Shari'ah law was replaced in Turkey by a Western-style legal system. Alcohol is freely available and many Westernised Turkish women live alongside women who wear a headscarf or a veil. Until recently, Turkish women wearing the headscarf were not allowed to attend Turkish universities. The charging or paying of interest on money lent or borrowed is perfectly acceptable. The way that Islam is practised in Turkey is more unified than it is in the UK. Many believe that Turkey has achieved the right balance between religion and society, but others have condemned it as betraying Islam.

Iran

Iran has a 98 per cent Muslim population and it is the only country in the world to be run by Shi'ah Muslims. There are nearly 49,000 mosques in Iran (in comparison with about 1000 in the UK). Virtually the entire community participates in Islamic worship and the whole of Iranian society is structured to accommodate this. In Iran there are also additional religious buildings called Hussainia, which are places to say prayers in remembrance of the martyrdom of **Hussein**.

A dual system exists in Iran: Shari'ah law dominates the legal processes and all laws passed in the elected Iranian parliament are checked to ensure they conform with Shari'ah Law. All legal decisions are made within the Shari'ah or religious law courts. The Iranian interpretation of Shari'ah law can be harsh, involving physical punishments such as beatings and executions.

> **The next two pages will help you to:**
>
> - explain how Islam is practised in other parts of the world
> - evaluate the differences between the way in which Islam is practised in Muslim and non-Muslim countries.

 **AO1 skills ACTIVITIES**

Give some examples of how Islam is interpreted and practised differently in other parts of the world compared with the UK.

Consider the different rights and freedoms which Muslim women can have in Turkey, Iran and Saudi Arabia.

In public all women are expected to wear a headscarf and a long dress. Polygamy (where men have more than one wife) is allowed in Iran and sex outside marriage is strictly forbidden. Boys and girls are strictly segregated at school once they leave primary school. However, Iranian women have taken part in major sporting events, they are educated and some have also entered politics.

Saudi Arabia

Saudi Arabia is a very traditional, conservative Muslim country. The country is run by the monarchy and its citizens have no constitution except the Qur'an. To preserve its Islamic nature, the country is closed to many new ideas and influences. For example, access to the Internet is heavily restricted and other religions such as Judaism, Hinduism and Christianity cannot have religious buildings of their own (although people are free to worship at home).

It is very easy to follow a Muslim way of life in Saudi Arabia because almost the entire population is Muslim. Prayer times and festivals are followed by the whole community and a halal way of life is easy to maintain. Two of the most holy sites in Islam are in Saudi Arabia, at al-Madinah and Makkah.

A strict interpretation of Shari'ah law exists in Saudi Arabia, where social religious law courts make all the legal decisions. There is a complete ban on drinking alcohol, gambling and homosexuality. Many regard the Saudi interpretation of Shari'ah and its punishments as extreme; punishments include the death penalty for adultery, the amputation of hands for stealing and public floggings for consuming alcohol.

Veiled Muslim women in Saudi Arabia.

Muslim women enjoy less freedom in Saudi Arabia than in the UK, Turkey or Pakistan. From the age of nine, all young girls and women must be veiled when appearing in public places. The sexes are completely separated after the age of nine, even up to university level. Saudi women have fewer employment opportunities than other Muslim women. Although women make up a very large percentage of university graduates they form only a small part of the workforce.

AO2 skills **ACTIVITIES**

Is it true to say that Islam is practised in the same way around the world?

In your own opinion is Islam a united or a divided religion?

Graded examples for this topic

AO1

AO1 questions test what you know and how well you can explain and analyse things. Let's look at an AO1 question to see what examiners expect you to do.

Question

Why is there a division between Sunni and Shi'ah Muslims?   **[6 marks]**

Such a question will be measured by the examiner in levels of response. There are three levels for AO1 questions, and the questions are worth 6 marks. The more detailed and relevant the answer, the higher the level and, more importantly, the better the mark. Remember the exam is about maximising your mark potential.

Student's answer

I think when Muhammad (PBUH) died there was a fight between Muslims. It went on for a long time but some wanted one man to be their leader and some wanted someone else to be their leader. So some chose one leader and others chose another leader. So that is why there is a split between Muslims.

Examiner's comment

This is a weak answer (*Level 1*). The answer has touched on the important point that there is a division in Islam which originated over the issue of leadership, but the point has not been developed or structured with any relevant information or detail. This student has failed to use any relevant key terms which would develop understanding.

Student's answer

Muslims divided into the Sunni and Shi'ah groups because they disagreed over who should be the next leader of the Muslim world when Muhammad (PBUH) died. The Sunnis believed the best person should be chosen for the job and Shi'ahs thought that Muhammad's (PBUH) cousin should have been the next leader. The Sunnis won.

Examiner's comment

This has now risen to a satisfactory answer (*Level 2*). The student has offered relevant information in a structured and organised way, but details are still lacking. A clear reason has been offered for the major split in the Muslim world. Key words have been used but better use needs to be made of them.

Student's improved answer

The major split in the Muslim world between Sunnis and Shi'ahs occurred over who should succeed the Prophet Muhammad (PBUH). During his lifetime Muhammad (PBUH) never made it clear who would be his successor or khalifah. The majority of Muslims felt the position should go to the best person for the job, they supported Muhammad's (PBUH) friend Abu Bakr and become known as the Sunnis. However, a minority of Muslims supported Muhammad's (PBUH) cousin Ali and they formed themselves into the Party of Ali or Shi'ahs. The Shi'ahs also believed that all future khalifahs should be the descendants of Muhammad (PBUH). The Sunnis won and this caused the split within Islam.

Examiner's comment

A very detailed and completed answer full of relevant information (*Level 3*). The answer is well structured and easy to follow. Excellent use has been made of specialist terms.

AO2

AO2 questions are designed to test your ability to present more than one point of view and to evaluate the different views. The quality of your answer will be graded in levels. The better the answer, the higher the level and the mark awarded (AO2 questions are worth 12 marks). A weak answer is often a one-sided personal viewpoint with very little supporting evidence or argument. A very good answer will draw on a range of different viewpoints, use relevant evidence and argument, and will be written in a very clear, easy-to-follow way.

Question

'Divisions help and do not hinder a religion.' Discuss this statement. You should include different, supported points of view and a personal viewpoint. You must refer to Islam in your answer. **[12 marks]**

Level 1

The candidate will demonstrate little understanding of the question. The answer will be too simple with little or no relevant information.

First show the examiner that you understand what the question is about. For example Islam is divided into two main groups, the Sunnis and the Shi'ahs.

Level 2

The candidate will show a little understanding of the question. Some relevant information will be included but often the answer is one sided.

Next go on to justify this point of view by referring to religious belief. For example, the split was caused by disagreement over who should be the Muslim leader after the death of Muhammad ﷺ. Sunnis believed it should be members of Muhammad's ﷺ family. As a result both groups follow different leaders.

Level 3

The candidate will show a satisfactory understanding of the question with a range of relevant material and appropriate evidence.

For the next stage, offer a deeper explanation. As a result of following different leaders, different practices have emerged in Islam. For example, when Shi'ah Muslims pray they must put their head on some earth or a piece of baked mud from the plain of Karbala. They also remember the martyrdom of Hussein during Ashura. Such divisions cause problems between Sunnis and Shi'ahs. Also offer a different point of view. However, most Sunni and Shi'ah Muslims get along with each other so each group can follow their own beliefs which has to be helpful to Islam. Offer your own opinion here.

Level 4

The candidate will show a clear understanding of the question with a range of fully supported viewpoints backed by relevant evidence and argument.

Finally, offer a deeper explanation of both viewpoints. You might mention that in Shi'ah Islam the Imams have the power to interpret the Qur'an. The death of Hussein at the hands of Sunni Muslims plays a major part in Shi'ah belief and practice and leads to division. In modern Iraq there is conflict between the Sunni and Shi'ah communities.

You might like to counter this viewpoint by saying that much unites Shi'ahs and Sunnis. Both groups accept the Qur'an and the key beliefs of Islam; they both follow the Five Pillars. Differences can be a positive thing in any community and can help to strengthen it. Finally, remember to offer your own opinion and explain why you think as you do.

These specimen answers provide an outline of how you could construct your response. Space does not allow us to give a full response. The examiner will be looking for more detail in your actual exam responses.

Remember and Reflect

AO1 Describe, explain and analyse, using knowledge and understanding

Find the answer on:

1 Explain, in one sentence, what each of the following words means:
   a *Sunni*
   b *Shi'ah*
   c *khalifah*.

PAGE 61

2 Why did the Muslim world split into Sunnis and Shi'ahs after the death of Muhammad ﷺ?

PAGE 64–65

3 Explain why the martyrdom of Hussein is important to Shi'ah Muslims.

PAGE 67

4 Outline the main features of the Shi'ah festival of Ashura. Why is blood such an important symbol?

PAGE 68–69

5 Design your own symbols which might symbolise Shi'ah Islam and Sunni Islam. Explain your symbols in words as well.

PAGE 70–71

6 List six ways in which Shi'ah Muslims practise their religion differently to Sunni Muslims.

PAGE 70–71

7 List six ways in which Shi'ah Muslims practise their religion in the same way as Sunnis.

PAGE 72–73

8 What are Fivers, Seveners and Twelvers?

PAGE 75

9 Explain who the Hidden Imam is.

PAGE 75

10 Describe the major divisions within the British Muslim community.

PAGE 76–77

11 In what ways is the British Muslim community united?

PAGE 76–77

12 Copy and complete the table below, listing different ways in which Islam is practised in the UK, Turkey, Iran and Saudi Arabia.

PAGE 78–81

UK	Turkey	Iran	Saudi Arabia

AO2 Use evidence and reasoned argument to express and evaluate personal responses, informed insights, and differing viewpoints

1 How could the Sunni/Shi'ah split have been avoided?

2 How might Sunni and Shi'ah Muslims put aside their differences, or are these differences too deep?

3 What essential beliefs make a Shi'ah Muslim different from a Sunni Muslim?

4 'The Muslim community in Britain can never really speak as one. It is just too divided.' Do you agree? What would a Muslim say? Give reasons for your answers, and make sure you consider a variety of viewpoints.

5 'Differences within a religion are a good thing.' Do you agree? Why or why not?

6 'A British Muslim would find it difficult to recognise their religion if they travelled to other parts of the Muslim world.' What is your view? Why?

7 'All members of a religion should forget their differences and worship together.' Explain your own view and those of others.

Your view	Muslim view	Another view

Topic 4: Places and forms of worship

The Big Picture

In this Topic you will be addressing the significance of Muslim places and forms of worship and how Muslims use features and artefacts as part of worship:

- the design of a mosque
- the absence of any representation of Allah or Muhammad ﷺ
- artefacts and features of a mosque
- private and public acts of worship
- the role of an imam.

You will also consider the ways in which the mosque is used by the community.

What?

You will:

- be able to explore the ways in which Muslim artefacts are used in the practicalities of worship
- explain the ways in which these artefacts may support and influence the belief and attitude of the worshipper
- make links between these places and forms of worship and what you think/believe.

How?

By:

- recalling and selecting information about artefacts used in practicalities of worship
- thinking about the relevance and influences on Muslim worship today
- evaluating your own views about worship.

Why?

Because:

- these aspects of practicalities of worship underpin the key importance that worship plays in Islam
- recognising places and forms of worship in Islam can help you understand the beliefs and attitude of how Muslim worship can be influenced and supported by the use of artefacts
- understanding these practicalities of worship helps you to compare and contrast how and where others worship, including thinking about your own view on worship.

1 Think of a celebrity such as David Tennant, a football club such as Liverpool, a fashion model such as Kate Moss and your school. In one way or another they can all be related to worship. Which do you think is the odd one out? Why have you chosen that one as the odd one out? What was it that linked the other three?

2 What do you worship and why? Now discuss with a partner and compare views.

The Mosque of Muhammad Ali Pasha (the Alabaster Mosque) in Cairo, Egypt.

Develop your knowledge

Places and forms of worship

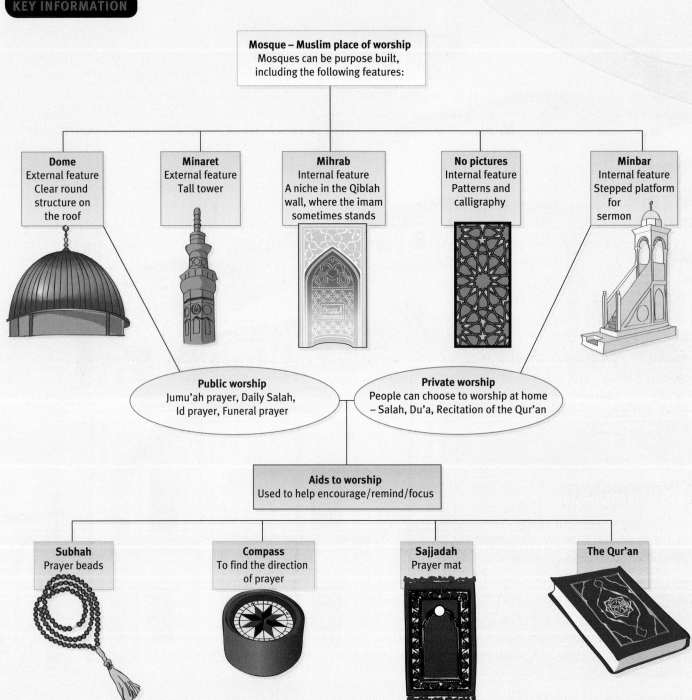

Mosque – Muslim place of worship
Mosques can be purpose built, including the following features:

Dome
External feature
Clear round structure on the roof

Minaret
External feature
Tall tower

Mihrab
Internal feature
A niche in the Qiblah wall, where the imam sometimes stands

No pictures
Internal feature
Patterns and calligraphy

Minbar
Internal feature
Stepped platform for sermon

Public worship
Jumu'ah prayer, Daily Salah, Id prayer, Funeral prayer

Private worship
People can choose to worship at home – Salah, Du'a, Recitation of the Qur'an

Aids to worship
Used to help encourage/remind/focus

Subhah
Prayer beads

Compass
To find the direction of prayer

Sajjadah
Prayer mat

The Qur'an

KNOWLEDGE AND UNDERSTANDING

What is a mosque?

What are the internal features of a mosque?

What types of different facilities does a mosque offer?

What is the difference between private and public worship?

ANALYSIS AND EVALUATION

Assess whether you believe a place of worship is necessary. Why do you believe this?

Evaluate why the mosque is significant to Muslims.

How can you relate daily worship to your own life?

Analyse the view that aids may help the worshipper concentrate and get closer to God.

calligraphy A style of decorative writing which is used to illustrate copies of the Qur'an.

du'a Varying forms of personal prayer and supplication.

imam A person who leads communal prayer, administers ceremonies and offers their communities spiritual guidance. In Shi'ah Islam, imam is also the title of Ali (Radhi-Allahu-anhu – may Allah be pleased with him) and his successors.

Jumu'ah The weekly communal Salah, and attendance at the khutbah performed shortly after midday on Fridays.

Ka'bah Cube-shaped structure in the centre of the grand mosque in Makkah. It was built by Ibrahim and was cleansed of idols by the Prophet Muhammad ﷺ. Muslims pray in the direction of this building.

khutbah Talk delivered on special occasions such as the Jum'uah and Id prayers.

masjid Place of worship (prostration).

mihrab Niche or alcove in a mosque wall, indicating the qiblah – the direction of Makkah, towards which all Muslims face to perform Salah. It helps the worshipper to remain focused.

minaret Tall spires with onion-shaped crowns, usually either free standing or much taller than any surrounding support structure.

minbar Rostrum; platform; dais. The stand from which the imam delivers the khutbah or speech in the mosque or praying ground.

mosque Muslim place of worship.

qiblah Direction which Muslims face when performing Salah – towards the Ka'bah.

Qur'an Allah's word revealed through Muhammad ﷺ to humanity; the most important holy book of Islam.

sajjadah A prayer mat which is a small and portable carpet that Muslims put on the floor when they perform their prayers.

Salah Obligatory set prayer five times a day; one of the Five Pillars of Islam.

subhah String of beads used to count recitations in worship.

ummah Worldwide community of Muslims; the nation of Islam.

wudu Ritual washing before praying.

Muslims practise both public and private worship. This helps the worshipper to feel that they belong to a wider community as well as having the choice for independent worship.

Explain why you think public worship might be better than private worship? Are there some things, or an act, that you do publicly and other things that you do privately? Why is this? What the advantages and disadvantages of doing these things publicly and privately?

The mosque

The Shah Jahan Mosque in Woking.

The mosque

The word '**mosque**' or **masjid** in Arabic means 'place of prostration' (bowing down with head to the earth before Allah). This also indicates that any place where a muslim lays a prayer mat, either at home or outside, becomes a mosque – a place of prostration. A mosque is a building that is a special place for Muslims to pray and worship Allah.

In Muslim countries the mosques are usually purpose built with designs featuring a dome and **minarets** clearly displaying the symbol of a crescent moon or a five-pointed star at the top. This makes the building distinctive and can be recognised from afar. However, in the UK not all mosques are purpose built and can be of any design or shape. Many houses, old churches and even fire stations have been converted into mosques and used as places of worship.

AO1
skills **ACTIVITIES**

Working in pairs, make a list of all the things which you feel should be part of a place of worship. Now try to put these in an order of importance. When you have finished this Topic, go back to your list and see how it compares with a mosque.

The significance of the mosque

The importance of the mosque is evident in the **Qur'an** and Hadith. It links the establishment of **Salah** (prayer) as a duty upon Muslims with the mosque as an essential part of Muslim society.

The mosque played an important role in the development of Muslim society, holding a central place in the cultural and social life of Muslims. Even today, it still has a great impact on the life of Muslims and is a focal point for the community.

> **Hadith**
> *Wherever the hour of prayer overtakes you shall perform it. That place is a Mosque.*

Mosques and the ummah

The role of the mosque is to unite and bring together the **ummah**. Therefore when Muslims came to live in the UK their first priority was to establish a mosque. The first purpose-built mosque in northern Europe was the Shah Jahan Mosque in Woking, England, built in 1889.

Today, in the UK, there are many mosques established for Muslims by earlier generations and these mosques enable British Muslims to link and hold onto their Islamic culture.

Types of mosques

There are many types of mosques, some of which are purpose built and have all the distinctive features (see Topic 4.2) whereas others are existing buildings that have been converted into mosques. In the past in the UK, mosques used to be plain and simple but as the Muslims prospered they were able to afford big buildings which were enhanced with Arabian styles and designs.

In 1977 the London Central Mosque opened in Regent's Park at a cost of £6.5 million. As well as a prayer hall which can hold over 5000 people it also houses the Islamic Cultural Centre.

The type of mosque that you will find depends on the culture and background of the people who worship there: a mosque in Ladbroke Grove, in London, has a beautiful open area with a large fountain which resembles Moroccan architectural design and the Sulemaniye Mosque in Hackney, London, features colourful patterns and designs from Turkey.

AO2 skills **ACTIVITIES**

'Every religion needs a public place of worship.' Do you agree?

What are the distinctive features of a mosque?

Entering a mosque

Before entering a **mosque**:

- Muslims take off their shoes as a sign of respect
- men usually wear hats and women have to be dressed modestly and wear the hijab (head covering)
- men enter from the men's entrance
- women enter from a separate entrance for women only, as mosques usually have a separate prayer area for women.

Features of a mosque

A mosque has many external and internal features, which signify a relationship between the building and worship itself. Some of the features are no longer used for their initial purpose, such as the **minaret** (calling people to prayer). This feature carries a historical link to early Islam and is still retained in mosques.

External features of a mosque include:

- The dome: The dome is a clear round structure at the top of the roof of a mosque which is usually visible from a distance. It is useful on an acoustic level for the **imam** to amplify his voice for the entire congregation to hear.
- The minaret: The minaret is a tall tower historically used by a mu'adhin (a person who does the call to prayer) to do the adhan (call to prayer). It is a distinctive feature of a mosque.
- Symbol of Islam: The symbol of Islam (crescent moon and five-pointed star) is usually found at the top of the dome or minarets. This is to symbolise a Muslim place of worship.

Internal features of a Mosque include:

- Prayer notice: Mosques usually have a prayer notice with five clocks, which indicate the prayer times for each of the five daily prayers. Some have extra clocks which, for example, show the time of Salat-ul-**Jumu'ah**.

 **ACTIVITIES**

You are to take your class on a guided tour of a mosque. Design a poster which shows a stop at each important feature with an explanation of what this feature is and how it relates to Muslim worship.

 **RESEARCH NOTE**

Do Muslims use pictures, or statues, as decorational features within a mosque?

- **Wudu**: This is a washroom area in which ritual cleansing is performed. Wudu it is a set sequence of ritual washing which all Muslims must do before performing their **Salah**.

- Women's section: In the mosque, women have their own entrance and section which is divided from other areas to allow them comfort and peace within their own surroundings.

- The main prayer hall: The most important part of the mosque in relation to worship is the prayer hall. The main prayer area is usually a large empty hall carpeted with prayer mats aligned in rows. This is an important feature for the congregational prayer as it allows the worshippers to stand in straight rows to begin the prayer. The prayer consists of bowing and prostration before Allah, so there is no need for any seating.

- The **mihrab**: In the prayer hall, people stand directly in front of a wall that is referred to as the **qiblah** (direction of Makkah) wall. Within the middle of this wall is the mihrab. The mihrab has a niche within the wall which allows room for the imam to stand and lead the congregational prayer. It is recognisable with its elaborate use of patterns and **calligraphy**.

- The **minbar**: A minbar is a stepped platform which is always to the right of the mihrab. It is raised in order for the imam to deliver his **khutbah** (sermon) usually on Jumu'ah (Friday prayers) or on any other special occasions.

- No pictures: A mosque strictly adheres to the rule of no pictures or statues to indicate the important belief of the Oneness of Allah. Muslims believe that the human mind is limited and is unable to depict an image of God – the Unlimited. Also any picture of Muhammad ﷺ would only amount to guesswork thus leading to a false image. Instead geometric designs and patterns with elaborate calligraphy are used to beautify the building. This leaves no room for any cause for distraction or a lapse for people to fall into idol worship. It captures the mind to the essence of constantly reminding them of Allah.

ACTIVITIES

'It is easier for a Muslim to worship in a mosque than at home because of the design and features of the building.' Do you agree with this statement?

The mosque as part of community life

The next two pages will help you to:

- examine the role of the mosque in the community
- evaluate how the mosque plays a central part in Muslim community life
- make links between the mosque and a place which makes you feel part of a community.

Facilities in a mosque

The **mosque** is the focal point of a Muslim community. It is far more than just a place of worship – it is a resource centre where sections of the community come together for very different events. As well as being a symbolic meeting place the mosque has many other functions such as:

Main prayer hall

Apart from the main purpose of **Salah**, the prayer hall also caters for other forms of worship and events:

- Id prayers
- **Jumu'ah** (Friday) prayers
- **Qur'anic** study circles
- solitude/meditation
- religious lectures.

After school madrassah

Many Muslim children attend an after-school madrassah at a mosque. Children attend the madrassah for an extra two hours in order to study and learn the Qur'an. They are taught how to read and understand the meaning of the Qur'an, the principles of Islam and how to lead a life in submission to the will of Allah.

Educational centre

Historically, for Muslims, the mosque has always been the centre for all learning and teaching and it continues to be regarded as such. Mosques are now more widely used as educational centres offering lectures and seminars to people of all ages, Mosques also provide people with a local community centre.

Weekend schools

Many mosques have set up weekend schools in order to enhance their community's education. These voluntary weekend schools offer extra support with Maths, English, Science, ICT and other subjects as well as Islamic Studies.

ACTIVITIES

Working in pairs, make a list of the things that you feel highlight the role of the mosque in the community. Now try to put these in an order of importance.

Library/reading room

A mosque has provision for a library and reading area for worshippers to come and use. It generally includes books on Islam and Muslim culture in order for Muslims to further their understanding of their culture and religion. Recent developments of the library/reading room include access to the Internet.

Youth activities

Some mosques, in order to attract and bring young people to them, provide facilities for youth activities such as ICT clubs and the establishment of football teams. This encourages the building of good relationships with young people and teaches them awareness of Muslim characteristics.

Young people are also encouraged to use the mosque as their social meeting place and to organise their own study classes and activities.

Women's section

Muslim women are encouraged to seek knowledge and also to socialise and interact. Mosques therefore aim to meet this need and a women's section is provided for all women to come together, to be educated as well as to socialise.

One reason for the separate section for women is (not because they are seen as inferior) the issue of the positions of Salah, because it is thought that if women and men prayed together the men might be distracted from their prayers.

Canteen

Mosques have a canteen for worshippers who attend the mosque after work or who go there to socialise. The facilities of the canteen, or restaurant, enables the mosque to provide food for weddings, events and also free food during the month of Ramadan (the month of fasting).

Marriage hall

Most mosques have a large hall, usually on the ground floor, which caters for events and, most often, weddings. Muslim weddings do not have to take place at a mosque, they can be celebrated anywhere, but those who wish to obtain a blessing from the mosque can hold their special occasion there.

Funeral facilities

Just as a birth is celebrated in Islam, likewise a death is also acknowledged with prayers and final goodbyes. Some larger mosques have a built-in mortuary. In preparation for burial, Muslims have to be washed in a specific way. A place to handle and wash the bodies is also provided.

The main hall, or a hall near to the funeral facilities, may be used for the funeral prayers although sometimes these are said at a cemetery.

ACTIVITIES

Evaluate why a mosque requires so many facilities which are not directly linked to worship.

Design a leaflet advertising all the facilities and activities offered at your school.

Describe some of the social activities that take place at a mosque. How do these help to strengthen the community?

Does the use of a mosque for activities other than prayer prevent it from being a holy place?

The use of artefacts in worship

The next two pages will help you to:

- identify the types and different ways that Islamic artefacts are used in worship
- evaluate how artefacts aid the worshipper.

These clocks show the times for the five daily prayers, and for Jumu'ah (Friday) prayers.

Aids to worship

Islamic artefacts help Muslims:

- to keep focus
- by reminding them of Allah
- to connect the mind, body and soul
- by engaging them to stop and think
- by encouraging them to worship and remain steadfast.

 **ACTIVITIES**

Are artefacts necessary for worship?

Features of a mosque as aids to worship

In Topic 4.2 we studied many of the distinctive features of a **mosque**, some of which are designed to aid the worshipper in the remembrance of Allah. Examples include **mihrab** which helps the worshipper to remain focused, **calligraphy** which engages the reader and fills their hearts with the words of Allah, and **qiblah** which focuses the mind on the **Ka'bah** (House of Allah) which in return connects the worshipper to Allah.

Other artefacts used in a mosque include:

- A compass to find qiblah: During **Salah** all Muslims face and turn towards the Ka'bah which is in Makkah, Saudi Arabia. The compass guides worshippers to the correct direction for prayer. Makkah is south-east of the UK.

- Time clocks: Salah is fixed at set periods and only changes according to the amount of daylight. In mosques there are often special clocks which show the times for the five daily prayers. Each day the clocks are changed as the time differs due to the change in daily sunlight. However, with the change of technology it is now possible to download timetables for the month ahead.

- The **Qur'an**: The Qur'an is the word of Allah and was delivered by the angel Jibril to Muhammad ﷺ who in turn memorised it and passed it down to his companions. The Arabic word Qur'an is derived from the word 'to recite'. Listening to or recitation of the Qur'an reminds and focuses Muslims on remembering Allah.

- **Sajjadah** (prayer mat): A clean place is one of the principle requirements for Salah therefore Muslims must pray in clean areas. The sajjadah is a mat that is used for prayer. The designs of the mat are usually patterns and pictures of the Ka'bah or the Prophet's Mosque.

- **Subhah** (prayer beads): The subhah is used as an aid to focus and concentrate on the remembrance of Allah. The subhah consists of 99 beads. It is used to recite the Ninety-Nine Names of Allah, the prayer after Salah and also for other forms of remembrance of Allah such as seeking forgiveness or thanking and praising Allah.

ACTIVITIES

Choose three of the artefacts of a mosque. For each one, explain how you think they would help a Muslim to worship and strengthen their belief. Which artefact do you think is the most important? Explain the reasons for your choice.

Preparations for prayer

The next two pages will help you to:

- examine the role of wudu
- explore the relationship between wudu and Salah
- evaluate why it is important to be spiritually and physically cleansed.

The purpose of wudu

The purpose of **wudu** is not just to cleanse dirt and wash parts of the body but also to wash and cleanse the body of sins that may have been committed. The parts of the body that are washed are hands, mouth, face, forearms and feet, and a wet hand is passed over the head. This refers not just to parts of the body which accumulate dirt but also to the washing away of sins that a part may have committed. For example, the gargling of the mouth to wash away bad words uttered, the washing of the face to remove lustful or wrongful glances of the eyes and also washing of the feet which may have led a Muslim on the way to temptation.

Performing the wudu

Wudu is performed with water but if there is no water available, such as in a desert, then sand is used. This is a symbolic wash which in Arabic is called tayyamum.

In order for **Salah** to be valid Muslims must perform the wudu:

- make intentions (niyyah) to perform Salah as part of worship to Allah
- wash the hands up to the wrists, three times
- rinse out the mouth three times (preferably using a brush)

Hadith Tirmidhi

The key to Paradise is prayer and the key to prayer is cleanliness.

ACTIVITIES

Explain why Muslims would need to wash five times a day.

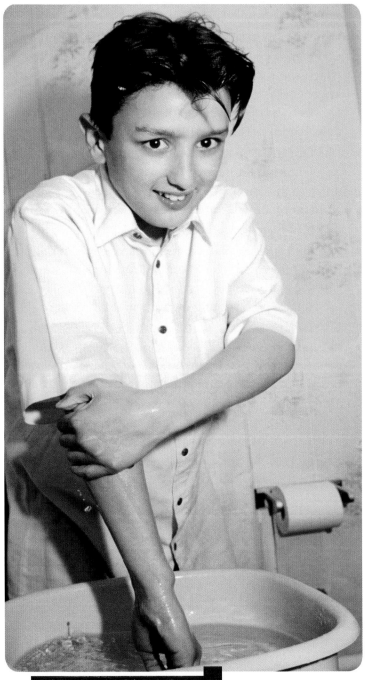

A young boy performing wudu.

- pour water three times into the nostrils, cleansing the nose by sniffling
- wash all of the face from forehead to chin and from ear to ear, three times
- wash the right arm from finger tips to elbow, three times, and then repeat the same with the left arm
- use a wet hand to wipe over the head once
- use wet fingers to wipe the inner parts of the ears with the index fingers and the outer parts with the thumbs once
- use a wet hand to wipe over the neck
- wash the right foot from the toes to above the ankles three times and then repeat the same with the left foot.

Completion of this ensures that the worshipper is ready to perform Salah.

Preparation for prayer

Adhan (call to prayer)

After the wudu has been completed the Salah is performed when the mu'adhin (person calling the prayer) calls the adhan:

The purpose of the adhan is to invite worshippers to join together in the worship and remembrance of Allah.

> *God is Great (×4)*
> *I bear witness that there is no God but God*
> *I bear witness that Muhammad ﷺ is the Prophet of God (×2)*
> *Come to prayer (×2)*
> *Come to success (×2)*
> *God is great (×2)*
> *There is no God but God*

Qiblah (direction of Makkah)

After all the preparations, the worshipper is ready to face Allah. In order for their Salah to be valid Muslims must turn to face the **qiblah** which is in the direction of the **Ka'bah** in Makkah.

ACTIVITIES

Design a poster showing a sequence of acts of wudu and explain why they are important and what they signify. Assess the view that in the modern age wudu is difficult to practise in the workplace. Do you agree? Give reasons to support your answer.

Public and private acts of worship in Islam

The next two pages will help you to:

- analyse the different forms of public and private worship
- evaluate the need for public worship in Islam.

Pilgrims at the Jamrah of Aqaba during the Hajj.

Public and private worship in Islam

Within Islam there are public and private forms of worship. This indicates that there are times when people must gather as an **ummah** to worship Allah and at other times, privately. Both forms of worship are as important as each other.

Types of public worship

There are many forms of public worship in Islam. They include:

- **Salah**: This is a form of public worship especially for men as they are recommended to attend the **mosque** for their five daily prayers (see Topic 4.7).
- **Jumu'ah**: This is a public form of prayer which is performed in a mosque or public space on Fridays.
- Salat al Janaza: This is a public form of prayer which must be performed for someone who has died (see Topic 5.8).
- Salat al-Id: The first of the Id prayers is given after the month of Ramadan and the second is given after Hajj, both are public forms of worship. These must be performed in a mosque or large open space after sunrise on the day of Id.
- Hajj: This is a public form of worship and the rituals of Hajj are all performed in Makkah (see Topics 2.4, 2.5). Muslims first stay at Mina and then go to Arafat. All Muslims performing Hajj must ensure that they stand at the plain of Arafat, collect stones from Muzdalifah, throw stones in Mina and perform tawaaf seven tims around the **ka'bah**.

Types of private worship

Islam requires believers to engage in private worship as this can help a worshipper to concentrate on God. There are many types of private acts of worship such as the following:

- Salah: The five daily prayers for women are performed at home and usually privately. Also all other voluntary prayers are done individually and thus in private.
- Charity: It is recommended that a Muslim excel in charitable acts such as helping someone in need; giving money to help the poor; volunteer work and setting up a mosque or school. These actions should be performed in private so as to avoid arrogance or showing off and the temptation to feel piety and greatness.
- **Du'a**: A private act of turning to Allah to thank or ask for help, protection, forgiveness or any other thing.
- Dhikr: A form of private worship whereby people meditate or recite forms of prayers, the Ninety-Nine Names of Allah, and seek forgiveness.
- Recitation of the **Qur'an**: During the month of Ramadan it is recommended to finish the recitation of the whole of the Qur'an as it is the month in which the Qur'an was revealed.

Hadith Bukhari

The believer's shade on the Day of Resurrection will be his charity.

ACTIVITIES

Consider the advantages and disadvantages of public and private worship. Draw up a table and then discuss it with the rest of the class. In pairs express your own ideas about the importance of public and private worship for Muslims.

'Charity should always be given secretly.' Do you agree with this statement? Explain how a Muslim might react to this.

Salah: a public form of worship

The next two pages will help you to:

- examine Salah as a form of public worship
- explore the different features of the five daily prayers
- evaluate the importance of Salah in Muslim worship.

Muslims gather to pray in the streets in Barcelona, Spain.

Purpose of Salah

The **Salah** (prayer) is an integral part of Muslim daily life. Although Muslims can pray and worship Allah at any time, it is compulsory for each Muslim to perform the five daily prayers at set intervals throughout each day. Any Muslim who fails to do this without having a valid excuse is committing a punishable act. This signifies that Salah is a very important part of Muslim worship.

Names of the five daily prayers

The five times for Salah are:

- fajr – morning prayer, performed just before sunrise
- zuhr – early afternoon
- asr – performed during the late part of the afternoon
- maghrib – performed just after sunset
- isha – late evening.

Muslims do not say Salah at sunrise, noon or sunset as these were times used by pagan sun worshippers.

AO1 skills ACTIVITIES

Name the different types of public worship in Islam.

Salah as a public form of worship

Salah can be performed at any place; either at home, the workplace or at a **mosque**. It is recommended that men, who are able to, must try to attend the mosque for the five daily prayers. The purpose of publicly performing Salah encourages the believer to remain steadfast and disciplined and also brings unity and a sense of community. Women however can attend the mosque at any time but are not required to do so.

The aims of performing Salah

The aims of performing Salah are:

- to worship Allah
- to unite people in the remembrance of Allah
- to enable people to get closer to Allah
- to become an obedient and devoted believer
- to cleanse worshippers of all wrong actions
- to keep worshippers from shameful, indecent and forbidden activities
- to encourage discipline and strengthen willpower
- to purify mind, body and soul
- to bring inner peace and tranquillity
- to show togetherness in equality, unity and brotherhood.

Conditions of Salah

Salah is compulsory for every Muslim who is sane, responsible and has reached the age of puberty. Parents are advised to encourage young children to start prayer before reaching the age of puberty so that they become familiar with the rituals and timings for prayer.

Validity of Salah

The Salah is invalid unless the following requirements are met:

Before performing Salah
- performing **wudu** (ablution)
- purity of body, clothes and the area of prayer
- dress according to Islamic etiquette
- declaration of intention to pray
- facing the right direction, the **qiblah**.

During Salah
- declaration of the greatness of God (taqbir)
- standing (qiyaam)
- recitation (qiraat)
- bowing (ruku)
- prostration (sujud)
- final sitting (qaida akhirah).

Voluntary Salah

This is a form of extra Salah which is voluntarily offered on top of the five daily prayers. The extra prayers may be to give thanks, ask for forgiveness, repentance or just to get closer to Allah. All prayers must be performed as if the worshipper was physically standing before Allah.

RESEARCH NOTE

Research the following terms related to Salah: rak'ah, ruku, sujud, tajjahud and qiyaam.

Hadith

Abu Huraira reports that he heard the prophet say 'If one of you has a river at his door in which he washes himself five times a day, what do you think? Would it leave any dirt on him?' The companions said 'It would not leave any dirt on him.' The Prophet said 'This is an example of the five prayers with which Allah blots out the evils of Man.'

ACTIVITIES

'It does not matter when you pray as long as you do it every day.' Do you agree with this statement? Explain how a Muslim might respond to it.

Surah 2: 238

Guard strictly your (habit of) prayers, especially the Middle Prayer; and stand before Allah in a devout (frame of mind).

What are the varieties of public acts of worship in Islam?

The next two pages will help you to:

- examine the nature of Salat-ul-Jumu'ah prayer as a form of public worship
- explore the different features of Salat-ul-Jumu'ah.

Muslims at Friday prayer in Bhopal, India.

The purpose of the Salat-ul-Jumu'ah

The **Jumu'ah** prayer is separate to the five daily prayers. It is a set weekly prayer which male Muslims must perform at the mosque as a congregation on Fridays. This is a public form of worship and cannot be performed individually.

AO1 skills **ACTIVITIES**

Remind yourself what the five daily prayers are and how they are different to the Salat-ul-Jumu'ah.

This is a compulsory form of prayer especially for men. Women are not obliged to attend because of other obligations they may have at home or with the family. Jumu'ah prayer falls on each Friday and is important because:

- it is ordained by Allah – as an occasion for Muslims to gather together and to worship collectively
- it is like a review of a person's weekly account of spiritual and moral actions
- it joins worshippers together in unity, equality and brotherhood
- it establishes the hallmark of obedience to Allah's command.

Salat-ul-Jumu'ah

The features of Salat-ul-Jumu'ah are:

- it is performed each Friday
- the time for the prayer is after zawal when the sun reaches its zenith therefore it replaces zuhr
- it cannot be performed individually and must take place in a congregation which is led by an **imam**
- if it is missed, it cannot be replaced but instead the normal zuhr prayer is performed
- Friday is not a day of rest, as on completion of the prayer people can continue with their day-to-day activities
- it must be performed at a mosque – if there is no available mosque then the congregation can be led at a different venue such as a home, college or an open space.

As with the five daily prayers, the adhan (call to prayer) is used to mark the beginning of Salat-ul-Jumu'ah and the congregation will start to gather.

Khutbah

Before the prayers begin there is a second adhan and then two short **khutbahs** (sermons). The imam delivers these from the **minbar**. The khutbahs are usually based on the **Qur'an** and Hadith. They are also based on topical issues which are relative to the area or situation of the community. The aim is to remind the worshippers and help them in their moral and spiritual conduct. The imam ends the worship with a **du'a** for the congregation and all of humanity.

Women

Women are allowed to attend Jumu'ah but are not obliged to. Some people say that this is not because they are seen as inferior to men but in fact because they have different roles to play. If it was made compulsory for all women to attend and if a women was pregnant or nursing her child it could be difficult. This gives women a choice to attend if they can but not commit a sin if they are unable to do so. If women choose to attend Salat-ul-Jumu'ah they pray in the separate women's section.

AO1 skills **ACTIVITIES**

Write your own sermon/speech on a current matter or issue which is relevant or important to you. Then in pairs deliver your speech to each other. How convincing did you find each other? Will you think about each other's speeches again and consider them?

What are the different forms of private worship in Islam?

The next two pages will help you to:

- examine the different forms of private worship in Islam
- evaluate the difference between public and private worship in Islam
- identify methods that a person may use in order to relax.

AO1 skills ACTIVITIES

Should worship be confined only to a private area or do you believe public worship offers other benefits?

A Muslim family praying together at home.

As well as public worship in the mosque, which is particularly important for men, and also the five set prayers every day, Muslims may also worship privately at other times so that they have an opportunity to feel close to Allah.

Du'a

Du'a is not part of a formal or set prayer and can be offered at any time, place and be of any length. It can be uttered in any language (it does not have to be in Arabic). A du'a can:

- be a private thanksgiving
- be a way of seeking forgiveness
- ask Allah for help, protection or guidance
- be a form of connection with Allah, attaining to seek His closeness.

> **Du'a**
>
> *Oh Allah, I have been unjust to myself and no one grants pardon for sins except You. Forgive me, therefore, in Your compassion, for surely You are the Forgiver, the Merciful.*

Recitation of the Qur'an

A private form of worship can also be recitation of the **Qur'an**. This is read aloud in a soft melodious manner to reach and touch the heart as a reminder of the words of Allah. The Qur'an can be read at home, the mosque or anywhere else and Muslims will usually then reflect and meditate on its meaning.

Subhah

Another form of private worship can be the use of the **subhah** to utter forms of praise and glorification of Allah, to seek protection or forgiveness. Usually after each prayer Muslims remain seated and use the subhah as an aid to say subhanallah (Glory be to Allah), Al-hamdu-li-llah (Thanks be to Allah) and Allahu Akbar (Allah is great) 33 times each.

ACTIVITIES

Devise a short du'a, including what a Muslim may use for an action such as asking for help with an exam.

'Reading the Qur'an is the best way for a Muslim to learn about their religion and to help strengthen their faith.' Do you think this statement is true? Give reasons to support your answer.

What is the role and significance of a religious leader in worship?

The next two pages will help you to:

- examine the role and significance of the imam
- evaluate the advantages and disadvantages of leadership.

The role of the imam

Islam does not have 'leaders' of religion or people in a hierarchy. The **imam** can be anyone who is qualified according to the Islamic principles such as anyone who:

- is a Muslim (not just from a particular race) and has a sound understanding and knowledge of the faith
- has a clear understanding of the **Qur'an** and Hadith
- has a voice which follows the recitation rules of the Qur'an
- is of good character and respected amongst his fellow Muslims
- is known for his piety and common sense.

An imam.

Today, unlike the past when most imams came from Muslim countries, there has been a change. Imams suited to a different culture were brought to Britain. This worked well as the earlier generations of Muslims were still in touch with their countries of origin and were able to relate to them.

Today these imams may be faced with many problems and issues which they have not been exposed to before, and this may create a gap between them and the British Muslims.

Leading the prayer

All Muslims are seen as equals so there is no room for leadership in the presence of Allah. The position of the imam is one who leads the prayer not necessarily as a leader.

It is a position which offers high rewards if practised correctly. However, there is also the risk of severe punishment if an imam is negligent or intentionally fails to perform their duty correctly. As the imam is someone who leads the congregational prayers he must be able to recite the Qur'an in the correct way.

AO1 skills **ACTIVITIES**

Write down what you understand the term imam to mean and then discuss with the rest of the class.

Helping the community

The imam is also an important figure playing a focal part within the community. He not only leads the prayer but with his knowledge of the Qur'an and Hadith he guides and teaches Muslims. He is available as a source of help and advice to the community.

The work of an imam

The role of the imam in the Islamic community includes:

- leading the set five daily prayers
- leading the **Jumu'ah** prayer
- delivering the **khutbah**
- conducting marriage ceremonies, funeral prayers and Id prayers
- educating and teaching people of all ages the Qur'an
- being an exemplar figure of Islamic character that follows the Prophet ﷺ
- offering sound religious advice
- visiting the sick and elderly and visiting Muslims in prison.

 **ACTIVITIES**

Devise a weekly timetable for the life of an imam – what different activities would he partake in?

	Sunday	Monday	Tuesday	Wednesday	Thursday	Friday	Saturday
Morning	*Lead prayer in mosque*						
Afternoon	Prison visit						
Evening							

Have you ever been a leader of anything (sports team, group work, or for example, as a captain or school representative)? Write down why your position was so important to the rest of your team.

Welcome to the Grade Studio

To get high grades in this Topic you will need to have a good knowledge of the structure and content of a place of worship as well as being able to show that you know how, and for what reasons, Muslims will use the place and the artefacts within it, in their public worship.

What sort of questions will you be asked? You can expect to be asked specific factual questions about the artefacts and the symbolic importance of the places of worship. You will be expected to be able to describe what goes on in Muslim worship and what it means to Muslims.

Graded examples for this topic

AO1

AO1 questions test what you know and how well you can explain and analyse things. Let's look at an AO1 question to see what examiners expect you to do.

Question

Explain the differences between public and private worship in Islam.   **[6 marks]**

Student's answer

The differences between public and private worship in Islam are that worship can take place at a Muslim home or outside such as in a mosque.

There are many differences between a public and a private place of worship as some people like to worship alone at home and feel more comfortable. Others like to go out to a mosque and meet other worshippers who may help them get closer to Allah.

In Islam the difference between private and public worship does not depend on the worshipper. This is because Allah has defined what worship takes place where and when. This applies to compulsory worship mainly. In the case of extra voluntary prayers, these can be done in public or private.

Examiner's comment

The student gave a basic overview of their understanding of the question with no use of specialist terms or detail (*Level 1*).

The student then moved on to explain further and give some relevant examples and used some specialist terms which earned a *Level 2*.

To reach *Level 3* the student would have to explain, using a clear detailed analysis, complete understanding of the question. This must include significant and appropriate specialist terms which are presented in a structured format.

AO2

Question

Worship should only be confined to a private area not public. **[12 marks]**

Discuss this statement. You should include different, supported points of view and a personal viewpoint. You must refer to Islam in your answer. This question is trying to test your ability to present more than one point of view and to evaluate them (AO2). Examiners will use levels to measure the quality of your response. A good answer will not only state a point of view, it will justify that view in some detail, drawing on religious beliefs and teachings.

Student's answer

I disagree because worship in public can help and be beneficial to a worshipper. There are benefits to praying in private as you can concentrate but public worship brings all the believers together.

Examiner's comment

The student gave an opinion and gave a reason for their view (*Level 1*).

The student then moved on to give good examples to support their answer and referred to another viewpoint, which earned the student *Level 2*.

To reach *Level 3* the student would have to explain both points of view in more detail, referring to religious or moral ideas about the statement, and give their own opinion.

To reach *Level 4*, the student would need to discuss the idea of public and private worship and how it might affect the worshipper. The student should also consider different views and give a personal response which is supported.

Student's improved answer

I disagree because worship in public can help and be beneficial to a worshipper.

There are benefits to praying in private as you can concentrate but public worship brings all the believers together.

Muslims will not agree with this statement as they have a mosque which is a public place of worship. Muslims have some worship which is specifically public and therefore cannot be done in private. Public worship can be the five daily prayers or the Friday prayer. This helps the whole Muslim community to gather together and worship and is a compulsory part of worship.

However other Muslims may agree because they feel that public worship distracts them and they can't concentrate. Also private worship allows them to be more intimate with God.

When I attend Church I meet lots of my friends and can worship together so I like going to the Church. Sometimes I also like praying in my bedroom as I can really connect with God. So I think that both private and public worship has many benefits for the worshipper and they should be given a choice. Either they can pray at home or go to the mosque.

These specimen answers provide an outline of how you could construct your response. Space does not allow us to give a full response. The examiner will be looking for more detail in your actual exam responses.

Remember and Reflect

AO1 Describe, explain and analyse, using knowledge and understanding

Find the answer on:

1 Using one sentence explain what the following key words mean:

   1 Mosque
   2 Minaret
   3 Mihrab
   4 Minbar
   5 Khutbah
   6 Wudu
   7 Subhah
   8 Sajjadah
   9 Qiblah
  10 Jumu'ah
  11 Du'a

PAGE 89

2 What are the distinctive features of a mosque?   **PAGE 92–93**

3 Why do Muslims not use pictures or statues in a mosque?   **PAGE 93**

4 Why does a mosque provide other facilities for worshippers?   **PAGE 94**

5 Do Muslims use artefacts in their worship?   **PAGE 96–97**

6 List the different aids to worship.   **PAGE 96–97**

7 What are the benefits of using aids to worship?   **PAGE 96–97**

8 Why do Muslims wash before each Salah?   **PAGE 98**

9 What forms of public acts of worship are there?   **PAGE 100–105**

10 Outline the aims of Salah.   **PAGE 102–103**

11 Explain the role of the imam.   **PAGE 108–109**

AO2 Use evidence and reasoned argument to express and evaluate personal responses, informed insights, and differing viewpoints

1 Assess how Muslims use the features of mosques and artefacts in their worship. How might these support and influence the beliefs and attitudes of the worshippers?

2 Analyse the role and significance of religious leaders in worship. Relate this to someone who has a significant role in your life and explain how this supports you.

3 Do you believe it is necessary to have a purpose-built place of worship? Why?

4 Evaluate features of different religious purpose-built places of worship and how they play a significant role in relation to worship.

5 'Religious communities should give their money to the poor; not spend it on building places to worship in.' Explain your own view and those of others.

Your view	Muslim view	Another view

Topic 5: Religion in the faith community and the family

The Big Picture

In this Topic you will be addressing Islam in the faith community and the family and consider the following aspects:

- rituals and how they reflect Muslim belief
- birth rites, the marriage ceremony and funeral rites
- nurture of the young and the role of the family
- private and public acts of worship
- zakah.

You will also consider the role and significance of religious communities to their members and the wider community.

What?

You will:

- develop your knowledge and understanding of the role of family in Islam and key family events and ceremonies
- explain the way in which these ceremonies reflect Muslim belief and portray and reflect the importance of family life in the community
- make links between the significance of these events and the important events in your own life.

How?

By:

- examining the key practices of these events and explaining their importance within Muslim family life (local, national, international)
- thinking about the importance of the role of the family and the relevance of ceremonies to mark these events in Islam today
- evaluating your own views about the significance of these events and the role of the family.

Why?

Because:

- these key events illustrate Islam in the community and the family and show how they reflect Muslim belief
- understanding these practices enables you to compare and contrast the strong emphasis of the role of family and ceremonies marked in Islamic events with your own life.

A Muslim wedding in Malaysia.

⏰ **GET STARTED**

Religious believers often mark special events in family life such as births and marriages. What special events have happened in your own life? How did they make you feel and why were they so important?

Religion in the faith community and family

KEY INFORMATION

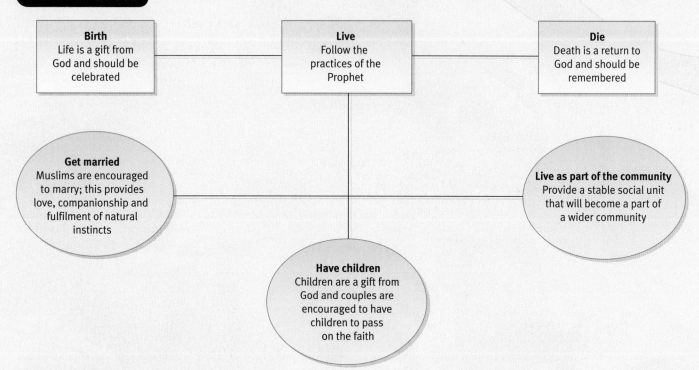

Birth
Life is a gift from God and should be celebrated

Live
Follow the practices of the Prophet

Die
Death is a return to God and should be remembered

Get married
Muslims are encouraged to marry; this provides love, companionship and fulfilment of natural instincts

Live as part of the community
Provide a stable social unit that will become a part of a wider community

Have children
Children are a gift from God and couples are encouraged to have children to pass on the faith

KEY QUESTIONS

KNOWLEDGE AND UNDERSTANDING

What are the different rituals that Muslims must follow?

What happens at a Muslim birth ceremony?

Are all Muslim marriages arranged?

Why is a family structure so important in Islam?

ANALYSIS AND EVALUATION

Why are Muslims not allowed to have sex before marriage? How does this relate to your personal views and why?

Evaluate Muslim attitudes to the roles of both husband and wife.

Assess the Muslim view on polygamy.

Have you given to charity or helped someone? How did this make you feel?

adhan Call to prayer by the Mu'adhin (one who makes the call to prayer).

Allah The Islamic name for God in the Arabic language. Used in preference to the word God, this Arabic term is singular, has no plural, and it is not associated with masculine or feminine characteristics.

aqiqah A ritual celebration and feast conducted seven days after a birth.

iqamah Call to stand up for Salah.

mahr A gift – usually money paid by the husband to the wife.

monogamy Having only one partner at a time.

nikah Traditional marriage ritual – the wedding.

polygamy A legal marriage of a man to more than one woman.

qiblah Direction which Muslims face when performing Salah – towards the Ka'bah.

sadaqah Voluntary payment or action for charitable purposes.

Shahadah Declaration of faith; one of the of the Five Pillars of Islam.

ummah Worldwide community of Muslims; the nation of Islam.

walimah The feast which follows a wedding.

zakah Purification of wealth by payment of annual welfare due; one of the Five Pillars of Islam.

 **FOR INTEREST**

'Sex before marriage is a sin and is not permissible in Islam. Hence marriage is recommended and should be practised.' Assess the advantages and disadvantages of sex before marriage. Do you think marriage is a thing of the past as more couples choose to cohabit? Explain your personal viewpoint.

Do Muslims have specific rituals that they must follow?

The next two pages will help you to:

- identify the different rituals of Islam
- examine how these rituals reflect Muslim belief
- evaluate the rituals (religious or non-religious) that you have attended and why they were so important to the people involved.

Rituals

In Islam, life is considered to be sacred and events such as birth and marriages are therefore seen as important and as gifts from **Allah**. A birth or marriage should be celebrated in order to thank Allah and share the happiness with close family and relatives. As well as happy occasions there are also sad moments such as death which should also bring people together. Muslims consider that all these events are there to remind people of Allah and to bring them closer to Allah.

Rituals in Islam are very important as they mark the main events in Islamic life which confirm, or reaffirm, obedience and the practice of belief. Each ritual marks a special occasion of the Muslim's life. These are:

Birth

In Islam the birth of a new baby is considered as a gift from Allah, and thus parents follow the traditional way in celebrating the new arrival. As birth is a new beginning it is begun with the remembrance of Allah. The baby hears the first words of the **adhan** which are 'Allah is great'. All aspects of the celebration reflect the nature of Muslim belief such as:

- Whispering adhan into the baby's right ear symbolises life begins with the declaration of faith (Shahadah).
- Whispering the **iqamah** – the call to stand up for Salah – in the baby's left ear shows the importance of prayer.
- The tahneek – rubbing a softened date in the baby's mouth – symbolises hope for obedience and a sweet nature.
- A head shaved of hair symbolises purity and a charitable act indicating thanks to Allah.
- The feast symbolises a charitable act to feed the poor and with the sacrifice of an animal they all show obedience.
- Khitan – circumcision which follows the Abrahamaic tradition and was the practice of the Prophet ﷺ.

AO1 skills ACTIVITIES

Working in pairs you have a minute each to talk about an event such as a birth ceremony, marriage or funeral that you have attended. Include what the ritual involved and why it was so important for the people who took part.

Marriage

Although Islam does not teach that marriage is compulsory, it was nevertheless recommended by the Prophet Muhammad ﷺ and therefore Muslims believe that it should be practised. In Islam, the Prophet Muhammad ﷺ is the greatest example of perfection in terms of worship, obedience and noble characteristics and he was married. So Muslims should marry if they are able to in order to follow in his example.

Although Muhammad ﷺ had several wives and Islam permits this, most Muslims live in monogamous relationships.

Bukhari Hadith
He, who is able to, should marry.

Death

Death for a Muslim is not the end, but rather a beginning of an eternal life. At the point of death Muslims are encouraged to utter the declaration of faith which seals their life. This shows that life began with the declaration of faith and at the point of death it is sealed with it. When a Muslim person dies it is recommended that they be buried as soon as possible. Each part of the burial reflects Muslim belief:

Dying person

- Declaration of faith – confirms their belief.
- Reading passages of the Qur'an – brings peace and reminds them of Allah.
- Face the body towards **qiblah**.

Deceased

- Ghusl (body wash) – formal washing of the whole body.
- Wrapped in white cotton sheets – white indicates purity and cotton sheets show equality as all people whether rich or poor take nothing with them and will return with exactly the same (this is the same clothing as is worn by men on Hajj or umrah).
- Salat al Janaza – a special prayer to ask Allah for forgiveness and mercy.
- Reading of passages of the Qur'an – ask for forgiveness and mercy for the deceased.

ACTIVITIES

Choose one of the Islamic rituals and assess why it is an important event for Muslims and explain how it reflects Muslim belief.

Design your own ritual for an important event such as birth, marriage or death. Include a sequence of the event, what each point signifies, pictures of the venue, guests, food and different stages. The ritual does not have to be religious.

Muslim birth ceremonies

The next two pages will help you to:

- identify the meaning of an Islamic birth ceremony
- evaluate the importance of having a religious birth ritual.

Having children in Islam

Muslims are encouraged to have children as:

- children are a gift from **Allah**
- a way to pass on their faith to their children
- it is recommended by the Prophet Muhammad ﷺ
- having children that are good and obedient can be a reward for the parents.

Becoming a Muslim

Muslims do not have a birth ceremony to *initiate* the baby into Islam but rather to *welcome* it into the family and religion. Islam teaches that a child is already a Muslim and does not require any form of initiation. Therefore the ceremony is a celebration and a form of thanks for the gift from Allah.

Muslim parents and their child.

Welcoming a new baby

At the arrival of a new born a father, or a male member of the family, takes the baby and whispers the **adhan** (call to prayer) in the baby's right ear and the **iqamah** (command to rise and worship) in the baby's left ear.

The significance of this action is to ensure that the life of the child begins with the declaration of faith and sets the right scene for its future.

The Adhan

God is Great (×4)
I bear witness that there is no God but God
I bear witness that Muhammad is the Prophet of God (×2)
Come to prayer (×2)
Come to success (×2)
God is great (×2)
There is no God but God

The tahneek

Like the welcome, the tahneek ceremony takes place soon after the birth. This is when a parent or close member of the family takes a small piece of crushed date or honey and either rubs it on the baby's gums or places it on the tongue.

This symbolises a sweet beginning with the hope that they will be sweet natured and obedient. After this ritual a prayer usually takes place.

AO1 skills **ACTIVITIES**

What sort of birth ceremonies do Muslims have?

Naming the child

Naming the child is an important responsibility, that lies with the parents and close family, as it is believed that the nature of the name reflects the personality and characteristics which the child will grow into. The Prophet Muhammad ﷺ recommended that parents carefully choose the name of their child to give them the right start in life. That is why almost all Muslims' names are carefully chosen and usually represent the family of the Prophet Muhammad ﷺ or his companions. Hence many boys are called Muhammad, Ahmed, Ali, or Omar and many girls are named Khadijah, Fatima, Aysha and Zainab.

Aqiqah

Aqiqah is one of the most important elements of the birth ceremony which takes place seven days after the birth. This is when a big feast is organised for friends and family. The aqiqah ceremony consists of many parts:

- Animal sacrifice: An animal is sacrificed as a symbol of thanksgiving. The meat is cooked and eaten at the big feast of the aqiqah and some will be given to the poor and needy, family, friends and neighbours as a symbol of thanksgiving for what Allah has given to the family.

- Shaving the hair off the head: The baby's head is shaved as a symbolic attribute of purity. After this the hair is weighed and the weight made up in silver, this money is donated to the poor. As the hair does not weigh very much, parents often give extra money as a symbol of thanking Allah for the gift of the child.

- Announcing the name of the child: The child is officially given its name and this is announced at the aqiqah ceremony.

- Khitan: If the baby is a boy, he must be circumcised, following the practice of the Abrahamaic tradition. This is where the foreskin of the penis is removed as a sign and confirmation of the Islamic Faith. If the baby is healthy this takes place at an early age. Although this practice may sound cruel it is often said to be beneficial for the health and hygiene of the child. Circumcision does not in any way affect or prevent a man from experiencing sexual enjoyment within a relationship.

AO1 skills **ACTIVITIES**

Write a letter to your friend explaining what happens at a Muslim birth ceremony. You must include all the different stages and what they represent. Why is it important to have a religious birth ceremony? What does your name mean and why was it chosen?

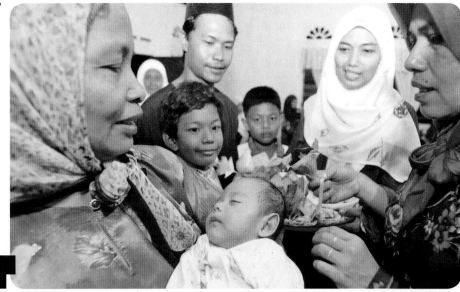

A Muslim birth ceremony.

Are all Muslim marriages arranged?

The next two pages will help you to:

- examine the ways in which Muslims find a suitable person to marry
- evaluate the Muslim criteria of choosing a partner
- make links between how Muslims find partners and the practice in other communities.

A Muslim marriage in London.

Arranged marriage

Arranged marriage is a term which is sometimes misunderstood and perceived as a 'forced marriage'. Within Islam there is no teaching that allows the element of 'force' in anything and especially not within the guidelines of marriage. According to Islam, marriage is a contract between two people who have agreed with free will and choose to marry.

If it was found that someone had been forced to marry the marriage is annulled because this is strictly against Muslim teaching.

For a Muslim to have an arranged marriage it means that someone (a parent, friend or other) introduces them to a person that they think would be suitable as a prospective partner for marriage. The reason and need for this sort of introduction is simply because Islam does not approve of young men and women who are not married meeting socially without other adults there. Therefore when a person is old enough to marry, family or friends help them find a suitable person to marry.

ACTIVITIES

Discuss with a partner what you understand by the phrase 'arranged marriage'.

Finding a partner

When finding a partner:

- Islam does not specify, or instruct, that all marriages must be solely arranged by parents. As long as Muslims adhere to the Islamic principles they can find their own partners through work, or introduction by friends or acquaintances.
- There are no restrictions in finding a partner from a different race. This is applicable as long as the man is Muslim and their children take the religion of the father.
- Men may marry any woman as long as they are Muslim, Christian or Jewish (People of the Book).

Choosing a suitable partner

When choosing a suitable partner:

- A marriage is seen not just as a binding of two people but also as a connection of two family units and must be thought-out carefully.
- A partner must be chosen carefully in order that partners remain loyal to each other.
- Questions must be asked to ensure they have common ground.
- Prior research of the partner's characteristics from their family members and close friends must be undertaken.
- The ideal for marriage in Islam is a life-long union based on trust, love and piety.

AO1 skills ACTIVITIES

Play the Halal dating game

- Organise yourselves into groups of six people: three girls and three boys.
- Imagine you are Muslims trying to choose the most suitable marriage partner.
- The girls are A, B and C – each pick one of the cards below and note down the details in your book.
- The boys must think of three questions to ask each girl in order to help you choose a suitable partner for marriage.
- The girls must answer the questions using the information from the cards.
- Boys should take it in turns to ask each girl their three questions.
- When all the boys have spoken to all the girls, each boy must decide who would be the most suitable partner.

Name: Aysha Malik
Family: Indian Muslim; parents now living in India
Profession: single Mum
Education: 4 GCSE's
Hobbies: shopping; going to the cinema
Looking for: kind, loving husband, who would help me raise my 3 year old daughter

A

Name: Hafsa Mitchell
Family: New revert; parents not Muslim
Profession: Hairdresser
Education: Degree
Hobbies: reading; travelling; going to Islamic conferences
Looking for: good Muslim man to help me become a better Muslim

B

Name: Ruqayah Sayed
Family: Syrian Muslim; living with parents
Profession: Uni Lecturer
Education: PhD
Hobbies: sport; research; cooking.
Looking for: intellectually stimulating man who is kind, loving and handsome

C

How do Muslims celebrate a marriage?

A Muslim wedding ceremony.

The Muslim marriage ceremony

Depending on which country, culture or tradition the couple are from, Muslim marriage ceremonies can last up to a week. The actual marriage ceremony itself is called the **nikah**. This is a short ceremony which comprises a sermon by the imam, vows, the consent and the signing of the contract.

Wedding venue

A Muslim marriage can take place anywhere and does not need to be in a religious place of worship such as a mosque. The **walimah** ceremony which is the feast and celebration is held at a different venue.

Mahr

The **mahr** is a gift from the groom to his bride and must be confirmed before the nikah. This can be of any value of money, gold, clothes or other items as long as both parties agree. The mahr can be given at the point of the ceremony or at a later stage and belongs to the bride. This gift belongs to the bride no matter what happens within the marriage.

AO1 skills **ACTIVITIES**

Describe what the following terms mean: bride, groom, nikah, imam, mahr, walimah and wali.

Imam

An imam (or any other respected and learned man) usually performs the nikah. He firstly confirms from each prospective spouse that the marriage is of freewill and consent. If the bride is not present then the wali, who is her marriage guardian, can respond (today this is not as common as the bride is usually present).

The Wali

The wali, who is the marriage guardian of the bride, is usually present alongside two witnesses throughout the ceremony. He also may be given the permission to act on her behalf if she is not present.

Vows

Vows are not compulsory but many couples do make them. Some couples also have written contracts before the nikah which state their rights and expectations of each other.

Marriage khutbah

The imam then leads the marriage sermon according to the prophetic tradition reminding the couple of the importance, purpose and value of marriage.

Readings

Often there are readings from the Qur'an. This passage from Surah 4 is often used:

> **Surah 4:1**
> *'O mankind! Reverence your Guardian-Lord, who created you from a single Person, created, of like nature, his mate, and from them twain scattered (like seeds) countless men and women – reverence **Allah**, through Whom ye demand your mutual (rights), and (reverence) the wombs (that bore you): for Allah ever watches over you.'*

Consent

The imam then asks both partners to say their vows and accept marriage in the presence of the witnesses. The consent of the bride is asked for three times, after which the couple are pronounced husband and wife.

Signing of the contract

The couple sign the marriage contract or licence, with witnesses observing. This validates the marriage legally.

Walimah

After the nikah the couples announce their wedding by having a party with family and friends. The party consists of a feast and also may include the playing of the duff (a musical instrument). The Prophet Muhammad ﷺ recommended having fun and enjoyment in celebration of such an occasion as long as it complies with the way of Islam.

ACTIVITIES

Using all the information and your knowledge gained on marriages, design a leaflet entitled 'Ingredients to a successful marriage'.

Or, in role-play groups re-enact a Muslim marriage ceremony:

- Firstly within your group, spend some time to sketch your role-play.
- Include a narration of how the couple met and background information.
- The ceremony must include all the different stages – mahr, marriage khutbah, vows, consent, signing of contract and walimah.

What are Muslim attitudes towards sex and sexuality?

The next two pages will help you to:

- assess why Muslims marry and how this relates to worship
- evaluate the attitudes of Muslims towards sex and sexuality.

An Islamic marriage

The reason why Muslims marry is because it is recommended by the Prophet Muhammad ﷺ. Humans have been designed in a manner whereby they need companionship, love, nurture, stability, kindness and affection. Marriage is such that it provides this security and curtails the sexual instinct that humans have. It creates a stable environment in which procreation can take place ensuring a good Muslim home.

Sex before marriage

Muslims do not permit the free mixing of the sexes and they encourage the use of segregation when children reach the age of puberty. This is to curtail their sexual instinct until they are married. Sex before marriage is considered a sin.

Sex

Islam recognises the needs and desires of human nature and outlines clear guidelines as to how to live in a lawful manner. Sex is natural and is seen as a gift and blessing from **Allah**, which is rewarded if within the boundaries of marriage. Within marriage, sexual intimacy is not just practised for procreation but most importantly for the increase of love and compassion between the husband and wife.

Muslims do not believe in celibacy. This is because suppressing or even resisting your natural instincts is not seen as spirituality and worship. Marriage and procreation are recommended.

AO1 skills ACTIVITIES

Why do Muslims marry?

Hadith

Whoever is able to marry, let him marry, for this will keep him chaste.

Surah 30:21

And among His Signs is this, that He created for you mates from among yourselves, that ye may dwell in tranquillity with them, and He has put love and mercy between your (hearts): verily in that are Signs for those who reflect.

A Muslim man with three wives.

Contraception

Throughout Islamic history temporary or reversible contraceptive methods have been used. Therefore, today some prominent Muslim scholars deduce that contraception can be used if:

- the mother's health is threatened
- there is a chance of a child being born mentally or physically disabled
- the family does not have the money to bring up a child
- there is a need to limit the number of children which people have in order not to damage their living standards and perhaps affect other children.

A Muslim family with many children.

Polygamy

Islam permits **polygamy** on the basis of fair treatment. Islam permits a man to have up to four wives. The laws laid down for polygamy are clear and ensure that all women have equal rights. For example, if a man has two wives, both of them should have their own place of residency and if one has a car so should the other.

Historically the practice of polygamy was to ensure that widows and divorcees (who had a small chance of remarriage) would not be left to live alone. Also if a wife could not bear children the husband would remarry but also remain with his first wife. Today the practice of polygamy is found only in some Muslim countries but the majority of Muslim marriages are **monogamous**.

Hadith

When a husband and wife share intimacy it is rewarded, and a blessing from Allah; just as they would be punished if they engage in illicit sex.

From Surah 4:3

'... *marry women of your choice, two, or three, or four; but if ye fear that ye shall not be able to deal justly (with them), then only one*'

AO1 skills ACTIVITIES

Using the information from this spread write a response to this letter.

Dear Problem Page
I am a 19-year-old Muslim woman. I have totally fallen in love with a man who is tall, dark, handsome and very kind. I could never have dreamt to have such a perfect match, we get on so well and he makes me laugh. We have been courting for nearly three months and he has asked me to marry him. I have accepted and the wedding will be set for next year in August. Now the problem is that he is getting too close. I mean he has started to subtly hint that he wants a kiss but I just laughed and turned away. But now he has openly asked me to sleep with him and says that if we are going to get married anyway it won't make a difference. I don't know what to do. What if I don't listen to him, he may leave me but on the other hand I am a virgin and if we do have sex and the marriage does not take place ... also what about my religion.... I don't know what to do please help!

In Islam are the husband and wife seen as equal?

The next two pages will help you to:

- assess whether Islam views the husband and wife as equal
- explore the roles of a Muslim husband and wife
- make links between the roles of a Muslim husband and wife.

Muslim men and women

Islamic principles clearly define and outline equality for both sexes; both males and females are seen as equals as they are created in pairs. Islam itself brought rights for women which the pre-Islamic era had not seen before. They were no longer inferior to men and were to be educated and skilled as were men. Men and women are equal except for their design and make up which inevitably gives both a different role. This however does not diminish their equal rights.

An example is that men by nature can be physically stronger, therefore enabling them to complete tasks which perhaps some women would find impossible. Likewise women are designed to be mothers, give birth and breastfeed whereas no man could possibly do that. Therefore it can be seen that it is possible for both genders to have different roles but be equal.

ACTIVITIES

Write down a definition of what you understand by the term equality.

> **Surah 36:36**
> *Glory to Allah, Who created in pairs all things that the earth produces, as well as their own (human) kind and (other) things of which they have no knowledge.*

Roles of women

Islam venerates women and encourages their fair and just treatment. Since the time of the Prophet Muhammad ﷺ, women have been leaders in their own right. Khadijah the first wife of the Prophet Muhammad ﷺ was a successful businesswoman, whilst another wife Aishah became a great scholar who taught men. Some of the greatest of the companions of the Prophet Muhammad ﷺ were also women.

> **Surah 33:35**
> *For Muslim men and women – for believing men and women, for devout men and women, for true men and women, for men and women who are patient and constant, for men and women who humble themselves, for men and women who give in Charity, for men and women who fast (and deny themselves), for men and women who guard their chastity, and for men and women who engage much in Allah's praise – for them has Allah prepared forgiveness and great reward.*

According to Islam every woman has the same rights as a man to:

- education
- worship
- spirituality
- religious duties
- life skills
- work.

This is continuously confirmed within the Qur'an which instructs every male and female believer. Both will have to fulfil each duty; live righteously according to the Islamic principles and will be judged by exactly the same criteria.

Role of a Muslim wife

A Muslim wife has the right not to work whilst her husband maintains her. However, if she wishes to work there is nothing in the Islamic texts which prevents or disapproves. A historical example of women working is the Prophet's wife Khadijah, who was a successful businesswoman. Clearly this shows approval for women who wish to work.

If a Muslim wife elects to work she can choose to support her family financially or keep the money for herself. Whereas when the husband works he must provide for and support his family.

If, however, the wife neglects her duties at home, which are to take care of food, children and her husband, then she is no longer permitted to work. This is because working is not an obligation whereas taking care of her household is.

Role of a Muslim husband

The role of a husband is seen as the protector. He is also the main provider and it is his responsibility to sustain his family.

A Muslim businesswoman.

Surah 4:34

Men are the protectors and maintainers of women, because Allah has given the one more (strength) than the other, and because they support them from their means. Therefore the righteous women are devoutly obedient, and guard in (the husband's) absence what Allah would have them guard. As to those women on whose part ye fear disloyalty and ill-conduct, admonish them (first), (Next), refuse to share their beds, (And last) beat them (lightly); but if they return to obedience, seek not against them Means (of annoyance): For Allah is Most High, great (above you all).

ACTIVITIES

Using the information from this spread, copy and complete the table.

	Muslim tradition		Another tradition	
	Husband	Wife	Husband	Wife
Role:				

Do Muslim family members have specific roles?

The Muslim family

In any society the family unit plays an important role in forming the structure of that society. So if all the families in a particular community were adhering to the same religious or moral principles, these would then set the foundations for that society.

In Islam the relationship of the husband and wife including their roles and responsibilities and the upbringing of the children are seen as the most important functions of the family. That is why so much emphasis is placed on choosing the right partner for marriage.

For centuries Muslim families have usually been extended and contained several generations, but today nuclear families are also more commonly seen. Despite this new development it is the duty of all families to take care of their young as well as elderly and disabled members of the family.

A Muslim family should provide a secure and stable environment which allows the correct human values and morals to develop according to Islamic principles.

Within the Muslim family it is traditional and seen as a duty for a man to go out to work in order to support his family. It is seen as the duty of the woman to bring up children and to look after the house. Also, in a traditional Muslim family, the man makes the main decisions.

However, the wife must be shown respect by her husband and children. The wife must protect her husband's property and be faithful to him. This model of the family is seen as the way in which **Allah** wanted men and women to live.

The next two pages will help you to:

- examine the nature of Muslim families
- explore the roles and responsibilities of family members
- evaluate why it is important to Muslims to have family values.

AO1 skills **ACTIVITIES**

Explain what you understand by this quote. 'O ye who believe! Save yourselves and your families from a Fire whose fuel is Men and Stones' (from Surah 66:6).

An extended Muslim family.

Parents conduct towards children

Muslim parents should provide their children with:

- a stable and loving environment
- adequate time for their needs
- the basic necessities of life
- a good education
- religious and moral principles
- an Islamic ethos in the family home.

Children's conduct towards their parents

In return Muslim children should:

- show respect to their parents
- look after their parents in old age as they looked after the children when they were young
- be considerate, loving, compassionate and merciful towards them
- be loyal and obedient (as long as it complies with Islamic principles).

A Muslim father and daughter.

ACTIVITIES

In small groups, using information gained about family life, work through the dilemmas below working out any possible solutions to the questions.

Amira is at secondary school. Her parents want her to wear the hijab as she is approaching adulthood. Amira loves to please her parents but is in a dilemma of how to face friends and school with the hijab. No one in her class wears the hijab. What do you think she should do?

Nazia has been avoiding any contact with Jason either during class or break times. The reason for this is that she is attracted to him. He is a great guy, good looking, great personality and has a good sense of humour. All ingredients to stir those young hormones. The science teacher has paired Jason with Nazia, to work on a project which requires after school meeting ... but the teacher knowing that Nazia is a Muslim has given her the option to change. Now her dilemma is whether to stick to Jason (as the whole class and Jason knows that they are partners) ... she could keep it strictly business ... will she be able to? Or should she just change? And what if her parents were to find out, how would they react?

Amir attends a secondary school where some people take drugs and have behavioural problems, but Amir likes his school and has a lot of friends. His parents are worried about how the school has deteriorated and that the effects of this might influence Amir. They have decided to transfer him to an Islamic school. Amir loves and respects his parents and knows moving school would please his parents, but he is in a dilemma as he will miss all his best friends and teachers and feels settled ... what should he do?

Imran's best friend Steve is having his 16th birthday party which will include alcohol, girls and no parents. Steve expects his best friend to be there. Imran is in a dilemma: if his parents find out he will be in a lot of trouble, what should he do?

ACTIVITIES

'Family gives mooring, an anchor, stability and tranquillity among close blood relatives and other family members' (based on the Qur'an). Explain what you understand this quote to mean.

What happens at a Muslim funeral?

The next two pages will help you to:

- examine the nature of Muslim funerals
- explore the different things that take place
- express your own view about life after death.

The dying person

According to Islamic teaching death is a return to **Allah** and therefore should not be feared. A dying person is encouraged to recite the **Shahadah** (declaration of faith). The family and relatives read passages from the Qur'an and prayers for the dead.

> **Surah 2:156**
> *To Allah We belong, and to Him is our return.*

After death

After death it is recommended that the body should face towards **qiblah** and the eyes and mouth should be shut. This signifies the essence of turning to Allah as in the case of Salah. The following are the steps taken to complete a Muslim Funeral.

Washing of the body

The first part of the ritual is the washing of the body. If the body is that of a male then it can be washed by the wife or someone of the same sex. If the body is that of a woman someone of the same sex washes them. The body is carefully washed with warm scented water according to Islamic principles.

Shroud

Once washed, the body is wrapped in white cotton sheets (three for a man and five for a woman); this is known as the shroud. The purpose of the shroud is to represent equality and unity.

Salat al Janaza (funeral prayer)

For the funeral prayer the body is taken to the mosque or an open space, where the prayer will take place. The funeral prayer is an important part of the ceremony as the worshippers, close family and friends will all join together and pray for the deceased person. Sometimes the funeral prayers are said at the cemetery.

Burial

Muslims do not believe in cremation and so all Muslim bodies are buried. The graves are dug according to Islamic tradition and the bodies are laid with the right side and head inclining towards the qiblah.

AO1 skills ACTIVITIES

Answer true or false to these statements.

- Muslims get buried.
- Muslims do not wash a dead body.
- Muslims must wait seven days before burial.
- Muslims get buried in their best clothes.
- The dying person is encouraged to say the Shahadah.
- There is always a funeral prayer.

Today in the UK, more and more commonly, Muslims are buried without a coffin as is done in Muslim countries. The reason for this is because humans are created from earth and should return to the earth. Therefore the body should be in contact with the earth.

As the body is lowered into the ground, the following words are said, 'In the name of Allah, (we bury) according to the Way of the Prophet of Allah'

'From the (earth) did We create you, and into it shall We return you, and from it shall We bring you out once again' (Surah 20:55).

This shows the belief that Allah will take the dead to paradise at the Day of Judgement.

Graveside

After the burial, Muslims believe that the person will be visited by two angels in the grave. It is recommended to recite the following prayer:

> *O male or female servant of God, remember the covenant (vow) made while leaving the world, that is the attestation (confirmation) that there is no God but Allah and that Muhammad ﷺ is the messenger of Allah, and the belief that paradise is a verity, that hell is a verity, that questioning in the grave is a verity, that the day of judgement shall come, there being no doubt about it – that Allah will bring back to life those who are in the graves, that thou hast accepted Allah as thy Lord, Islam as thy religion, Muhammad ﷺ as thy prophet, the Qur'an as thy guide, the Ka'bah as thy direction to turn for the service of worship and that all believers are thy brethren (brothers). May Allah keep thee firm in this trail.*

There should not be any large monuments in a Muslim cemetery; rich and poor are alike in death. Tombstones should just have the name of the person on them because Muslims believe that money should be given to the poor rather than spent on large funeral monuments. Usually the grave is raised just above the ground so that people do not walk or sit on it.

Mourning

To show feelings of sadness at the loss of a deceased person is permissible, as the Prophet Muhammad ﷺ himself wept at the death of his son. This is human nature but to wail and scream and question 'why?' is not recommended as death is a return to Allah, at a time which is appointed by Allah.

The period of mourning usually lasts from the first three days (which includes the burial) to sometimes up to the first forty days after the burial. During this time the families read and recite passages from the Qur'an, pray and ask Allah to forgive and be merciful towards them.

AO2 skills ACTIVITIES

Have a class debate on the following topics. Do you think it is better to be buried or cremated? Is there an afterlife? Do you believe in heaven and hell?

Why do Muslims give zakah?

The next two pages will help you to:

- examine the nature of zakah
- evaluate the reasons why Muslims must give zakah
- identify the benefits of zakah for Muslims and relate this to a good action that you have done.

Zakah being given to the poor.

Zakah

Zakah is one of the Five Pillars of Islam which Muslims must abide by. It is an important Pillar which not only relates to personal benefit and gain but also helps wider society as a whole. Wealth is a gift from **Allah** which is given to whom Allah wills; therefore it must be used wisely and according to Islamic principles.

Zakah is not just the mere offering of money but also contains many aspects of worship, all intertwined into one. These aspects involve the practical understanding of zakah as a duty upon every Muslim, alongside the moral and spiritual understanding of righteousness, kindness and generosity. On a spiritual level zakah helps to eradicate traits of selfishness and greed.

 **ACTIVITIES**

'Concern for the poor is the most important teaching in Islam.' Do you agree with this statement? Explain what Muslims might say.

The rate of zakah

It is compulsory for all Muslims who have wealth to give part of their income as zakah. This will purify their property as well as their heart. At the end of each lunar year each Muslim should evaluate their wealth and give a minimum of 2.5 per cent of surplus income to zakah.

Muslims who are eligible to receive zakah

Muslims who are eligible to receive zakah are mentioned in the Qur'an. This can be any Muslim who fits into the following categories.

- poor Muslims
- needy Muslims – to provide them with help and support which in return would help them to earn for themselves
- Muslim converts – to settle them into their new lifestyle
- Muslim prisoners of war – to release them with a ransom
- Muslims in debt – to relieve them of their pressures
- Muslim scholars or teachers – to help them with further research and study.

> **Surah 9:60**
>
> *Alms are for the poor and the needy, and those employed to administer the (funds); for those whose hearts have been (recently) reconciled (to Truth); for those in bondage and in debt; in the cause of Allah; and for the wayfarer: (thus is it) ordained by Allah, and Allah is full of knowledge and wisdom.*

Sadaqah

This is a voluntary action of giving to charity. Unlike zakah, it can take place at any time. **Sadaqah** is neither compulsory nor has a set fixed amount which is payable by every Muslim. It is a charitable act which can be of any nature such as money, kind words, helping people in need or even a smile.

> **Surah 2:274**
>
> *Those who (in charity) spend of their goods by night and by day, in secret and in public, have their reward with their Lord: on them shall be no fear, nor shall they grieve.*

RESEARCH NOTE

Research the work of a Muslim charity and explain how they operate.

ACTIVITIES

At the end of the year you realise that you have £10,000 and you need to pay zakah. Look at the people below and decide how much you will distribute and to whom and explain why.

'I am a young Muslim man who needs your money in order to buy the latest Xbox.'

'Please help me: my land is barren because I do not have enough money to buy seeds to grow crops which I could then go on to sell.'

'I am a widow with four hungry children. I am all alone, no family, my husband used to earn some money but now that he has gone – we have nothing!'

'I am in serious debt, I have lost everything that I have owned through my gambling and drug habit, I need some money to pay someone back, otherwise I lose my house.'

'I am a prominent Muslim scholar, and I teach and propagate Islam all around the world. I need some money to pursue research for my new book.'

Religious communities

The next two pages will help you to:

- explain the role of religious communities in the lives of their members
- evaluate the significance of religious communities to the wider community
- identify the role of your own community.

The ummah

Islam prohibits all types of prejudice and discrimination. It places strong emphasis on the unification of Muslims with disregard to race, colour, status, class or country of origin. All Muslims are regarded as brothers and sisters and so they are all part of the **ummah**. This builds solidarity amongst the believers and the Muslim community as a whole in enabling them to gain strength in unification of the Oneness of **Allah**.

ACTIVITIES

What is the role and responsibility of the ummah?

The work of the ummah

The role of the ummah is to support the whole Muslim community. The purpose of the work is to strengthen the bond between Muslims and to focus on their welfare and wellbeing.

The Pillars of Islam, and therefore worship itself, clearly propagate the importance of the ummah:

- **Shahadah**: unites all in the Oneness of Allah and belief in the Prophet
- Salah: recommended praying in the mosque, highlighting the coming together of the ummah publicly
- **zakah**: this is financial help and support for the needy or poor of the ummah
- sawm: unity in worship
- Hajj: an important event which displays the meaning of ummah – it brings Muslims together from all over the world.

Hadith Muslim
Believers are like the parts of a building; each part supports the others.

The ummah and other religious communities

The verse on the right clearly indicates that everyone should have choice and freewill to practise religion. Although in Islam, the ummah is a strong community, it still allows room for other faiths to live within the Muslim community and practise their faith. For example, in some Muslim countries you will see churches, synagogues and the community of non-Muslims living side by side with Muslims.

From Surah 2:256
Let there be no compulsion in religion.

The ummah and the wider community

It is important for Muslims to interact and integrate with the wider community because it is a duty for Muslims to propagate Islam. This is not to force people to convert but to make them aware of Islam and its lifestyle.

Muhammad ﷺ was sent as a 'mercy to humanity' not only to Muslims. So it is important for Muslims to treat all people as they would wish to be treated and never to judge a person on the basis of their faith.

The core and meaning of Islam is 'peace' and therefore Muslims should remain peaceful and respectful towards all of creation. Islam teaches that Muslims are khalifahs sent as stewards and trustees of the earth. Muslims should fulfil their obligation and co-operate in doing that which is pleasing to Allah.

The ummah in the UK

If Muslims choose to live in a non-Muslim community, they must show good conduct as this was the practice of the Prophet ﷺ. They should have good manners and principles which confirm Islam.

However, Muslims must adhere to the Islamic way of life and follow its rules and show obedience to Allah. This may be a challenge for Muslims to do but they must take positive steps to try to ensure that things are morally right.

Hadith

The messenger of Allah said: If you see an evil action, change it with your hand [i.e. Positive action]; or if you are not able to do this; then with your tongue; or if you are not able to do this; then with your heart.

ACTIVITIES

Using the information from this spread, copy and complete the table below. Choose a community that you belong to, it can be religious or not (youth clubs, school).

The Muslim ummah	Your community
Background information about the ummah	Background information about your community
Roles/responsibilities	Roles/responsibilities
Work of the ummah	Work of your community
The ummah and the wider society	Your community and the wider society

GradeStudio

Welcome to the Grade Studio

This Topic is about how the lives of Muslims are affected by their faith.

Graded examples for this topic

AO1

AO1 questions test what you know and how well you can explain and analyse things. Let's look at an AO1 question to see what examiners expect you to do.

Question

Explain why practising rituals is important to Muslims.   **[6 marks]**

Student's answer

Muslims believe that rituals are important as they are ordained by God or were practised by Muhammad (PBUH) who is an exemplar, who Muslims must follow.
This helps Muslims to be good worshippers and follow their religion. It also teaches how to behave and what to do as and when. An example is when a baby is born it is a time of great joy for the parents and family. Children are considered a gift from God, so Muslims have to in return thank God for His Gift by completing the rituals of a Birth ceremony. Unlike Christianity the birth ceremony is not done to initiate the child into the religion but rather to welcome and celebrate it into the family. Therefore rituals are very important and form part of the Muslim Tradition.

Examiner's comment

The student gave a basic overview of their understanding of the question with no use of specialist terms or enough detail (*Level 1*). The student then moved on to explain further and give some relevant examples and used some specialist terms which earned the student a *Level 2*.
To reach *Level 3* the student would have to explain using a clear detailed analysis with a complete understanding of the question. This must include significant and appropriate specialist terms to be presented in a structured format.

Student's improved answer

Muslims believe that rituals are important as they are ordained by God or were practised by Muhammad (PBUH) who was an exemplar, who Muslims must follow.

This helps Muslims to be good worshippers and follow their religion. It also teaches how to behave and what to do as and when. An example is when a baby is born it is a time of great joy for the parents and family. Children are considered a gift from God, so Muslims have to in return thank God for His Gift by completing the rituals of a Birth ceremony. Unlike Christianity the birth ceremony is not done to initiate the child into the religion but rather to welcome and celebrate it into the family. Therefore rituals are very important and form part of the Muslim Tradition.

Other rituals that are important for Muslims to practise is the marriage ceremony and the funeral. The marriage ceremony is very important as it is recommended by the Prophet (PBUH) who explains that marriage is half of religion. This is because sex before marriage is not allowed and is only permitted within marriage. Also the role of the family is very important in Islam therefore marriage is important. This is because family provides love, comfort, and care for the young and old. It is the basis for procreation and bringing up sound Muslims with good manners and morals in a stable environment. This then creates stability and a structured society.

Therefore we have learnt that rituals are very important and by Muslims practising them they are following the Muslim tradition. This is important so that they can live a happy life on Earth and a eternal life in Heaven.

AO2

Question

'Sex before marriage is the key to a successful marriage.' *Discuss this statement. You should include different,* *supported points of view and a personal viewpoint. You must refer to Islam in your answer.* **[12 marks]**

This question is trying to test your ability to present more than one point of view and to evaluate them (AO2). Examiners will use levels to measure the quality of your response. A good answer will not only state a point of view, it will justify that view in some detail, drawing on religious beliefs and teachings. At the highest level, an answer will also look at the implications of these points of view for society as a whole.

Student's answer

I agree sex before marriage allows the couple to gain experience and be better in bed.

Therefore this will help couples when they get married to enjoy sexual intimacy and also start a family when they are ready. Now, if a couple waited to have sex after marriage then they might not enjoy it and the marriage will end in divorce.

Muslims will not agree to this statement as they believe that they are not allowed to have sex before marriage. It is regarded as a sin and Muslims are told not to be in private with the opposite sex as satan will be the third which means that they may fall into temptation. They are recommended to marry as was the Prophet (PBUH) and should follow his example. Marriage allows sexual intimacy which is then considered a gift from Allah. Also they believe sex before marriage creates instability in families, increase in sexual promiscuity, unwanted pregnancies and could lead to STDs.

I can understand the Muslim point of view as in my area teenage pregnancy is on the increase. Also there is more peer pressure to have sex which could lead to someone losing their virginity and then later regretting it. But the problem is more and more people are not getting married, should they not have sex? My Mum had me when she wasn't married to my dad, so that doesn't mean that we have an unstable family. I do believe there are dangers in sex before marriage and you can catch STDs but you just have to be careful.

Overall, I believe that sex before marriage is a good thing and will help make a successful marriage. You will be more experienced and had all the fun with different people and can settle down to marriage with someone you love forever. It should be up to the individual whether they want to have sex before marriage.

Examiner's comment

The student gave a personal opinion and gave a reason for their point of view (*Level 1*).

The student then moved on to give good examples to support their answer and referred to another viewpoint, which earned the student a *Level 2*.

To reach *Level 3* the student would have to explain both points of view in more detail, referring to religious or moral ideas about the statement and give a personal response.

To reach *Level 4*, the student would need to discuss thoroughly the idea of sex before marriage and how it might affect the couple and society. The student should also consider different views and give a personal response which is supported.

These specimen answers provide an outline of how you could construct your response. Space does not allow us to give a full response. The examiner will be looking for more detail in your actual exam responses.

Remember and Reflect

AO1 Describe, explain and analyse, using knowledge and understanding

Find the answer on:

1 Using one sentence to explain what the following words mean
  1 Adhan
  2 Aqiqah
  3 Khitan
  4 Nikah
  5 Imam
  6 Mahr
  7 Walimah
  8 Polygamy.

PAGE 117, 118, 125

2 Name two rituals that Muslims must follow.

PAGE 118–119

3 Describe the Muslim birth ceremony.

PAGE 120–121

4 How do Muslims find a suitable partner to marry?

PAGE 122–123

5 Can Muslims have a love marriage or are they all arranged?

PAGE 122–123

6 Do Muslims have to marry?

PAGE 119

7 What do Muslims believe about sex?

PAGE 126–127

8 Is sex dirty and unclean and only for procreation?

PAGE 126

9 Explain the role of a Muslim wife.

PAGE 129

10 Do the members of Muslim families have specific roles?

PAGE 130–131

11 Why are prayers necessary for a Muslim who has died?

PAGE 132–133

12 What is the ummah?

PAGE 136–137

AO2 Use evidence and reasoned argument to express and evaluate personal responses, informed insights, and differing viewpoints

1 Why do people think it is important to follow specific rituals? Explain your answer.

2 Do you believe that there should be such a thing as a polygamous marriage? Why?

3 What could be the benefits of a polygamous marriage for both the husband and wife?

4 Assess the need and importance of marriage in Islam and relate this to whether you would ever consider getting married?

5 Evaluate the various different methods of burial.

6 'Religious people should always put their own families first.' Explain your own view and those of others.

Your view	Muslim view	Another view

Topic 6: Sacred writings

The Big Picture

In this Topic you will:

- explore the nature of the Qur'an, Hadith and Sunnah and their importance to Muslims
- consider why the Qur'an is the most important sacred text for Muslims
- explore how and why the Hadith and Sunnah are used
- examine how Muslims use the Qur'an in public and private worship.

What?

You will:

- explore how and why the Qur'an came into being
- understand what the Hadith and Sunnah are and how they are used by Muslims
- understand how the Qur'an is used in Islam as a source of belief and practice
- evaluate how and why the Qur'an is treated with great respect in Islam.

How?

By:

- examining the origins and nature of the Qur'an
- understanding the importance of the Qur'an
- evaluating your own views about the role and importance of sacred writings.

Why?

Because:

- it is important to understand the place of scripture in religion and its influence on belief and practice
- Muslims see the Qur'an as the single most important part of their religion.

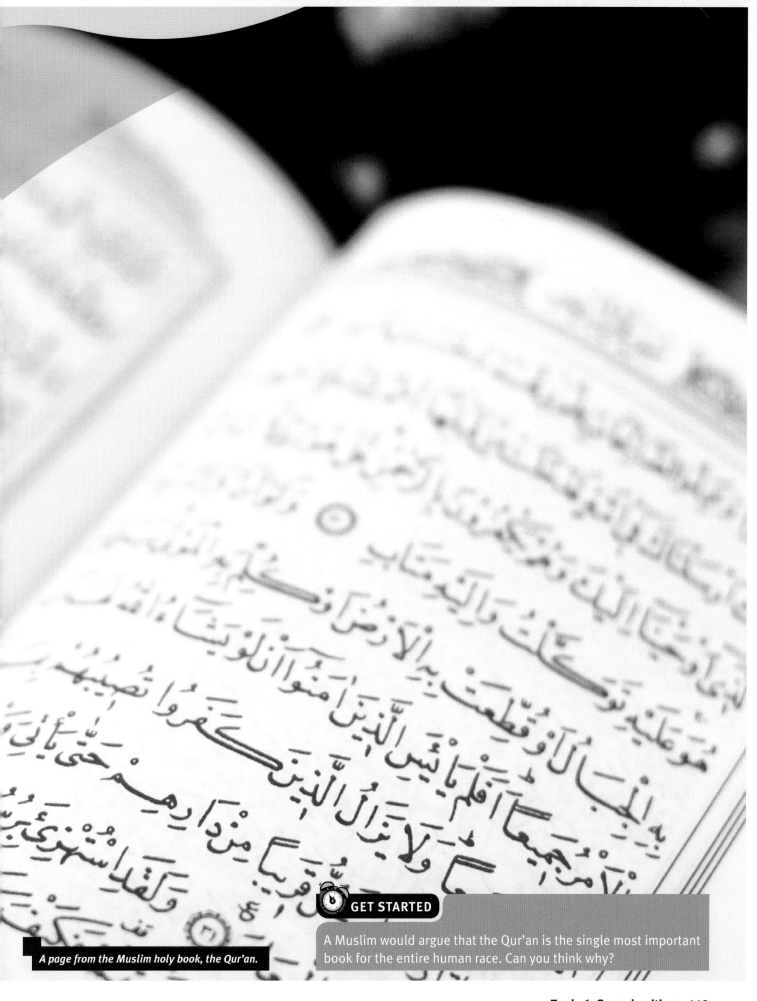

A page from the Muslim holy book, the Qur'an.

🕐 **GET STARTED**

A Muslim would argue that the Qur'an is the single most important book for the entire human race. Can you think why?

Develop your knowledge

Sacred writings

In this Topic you are expected to grasp the importance of sacred writings in Islam. You are expected to know and understand the following:

- The Qur'an is the most important sacred writing in Islam since it is the actual word of Allah. Secondary sources exist in the form of the Hadith, which are the sayings of the Prophet Muhammad ﷺ and the Sunnah which are the actions of the Prophet.

- The Qur'an was revealed to the Prophet Muhammad ﷺ in a series of revelations lasting 23 years.

- The Qur'an contains Allah's final instructions to the human race, since earlier sacred writings had been lost or changed.

- The Qur'an is not a book with a beginning, middle and end, rather it is a collection of revelations.

- The Qur'an was not organised into its current form until 20 years after the Prophet's ﷺ death.

- The Qur'an is the main source for Muslim belief and practice.

- The words of the Qur'an cannot be challenged.

- Modern copies of the Qur'an have to be exactly the same as the earliest copies to ensure accuracy.

- Muslims who have memorised the whole of the Qur'an are called hafiz.

- The Qur'an is at the heart of Shari'ah Law. Shari'ah Law is a system of laws which have evolved to follow an Islamic way of life.

- The Qur'an is central to many acts of public and private worship in Islam.

- The Hadith are secondary sacred writings which contain the things which the Prophet Muhammad ﷺ said.

- There are different forms of the Hadith available, the accuracy of some of them have been called into question.

- The Sunnah is a collection of things which the Prophet did.

- The Hadith and Sunnah are used to give further guidance on what the Qur'an says.

- Tremendous respect is shown towards the Qur'an in everyday life.

KEY QUESTIONS

KNOWLEDGE AND UNDERSTANDING

What are the main sacred writings of Islam?

Explain how Muhammad ﷺ received the Qur'an?

Why did it become necessary to put the Qur'an into its current book form?

Why is the Qur'an so important to Muslims?

How does the Qur'an influence belief and practice in Islam?

How and why is the Qur'an respected in a Muslim community?

What are the Hadith and how are they used?

What problems do some of the Hadith present?

Explain what the Sunnah is and how it is used?

How is the Qur'an used in public and private worship?

ANALYSIS AND EVALUATION

How far can Muslims trust the writings in the Qur'an and the Hadith?

Consider the role and importance of sacred writings in Islam.

al-Fatihah The name given to the first chapter or Surah of the Qur'an. It follows the form of a prayer.

calligraphy A style of decorative writing which is used to illustrate copies of the Qur'an.

Hadith A collection of sayings of the Prophet Muhammad ﷺ which Muslims consult to help guide them in their understanding.

Hadith of Ali Shi'ah Muslims have a collection of Hadith from their leader who was Ali, Muhammad's ﷺ cousin.

Hadith of Bukhari A version of the Hadith compiled by a Muslim scholar named Muhammad ibn Ismail. These are considered to be the most accurate Hadiths attributed to Muhammad ﷺ.

Hadith Qudsi Hadiths which were spoken by Muhammad ﷺ but came directly from Allah. They are considered the most sacred Hadiths.

hafiz A Muslim who is able to memorise the Qur'an by heart. Such individuals are given much honour in a Muslim community.

Night of Power The night when the first part of the Qur'an was revealed to the Prophet Muhammad ﷺ.

Qur'an Allah's word revealed through Muhammad ﷺ to humanity; the most important holy book of Islam.

Sahih al-Bukhari A collection of Hadith made by Muhammad ibn Ismail. He was born in Bukhara. These are believed to be the most genuine Hadith.

Sunnah Model practices, customs and traditions of Muhammad ﷺ.

Surah A chapter in the Qur'an. There are 114 of these arranged from longest to shortest.

Uthman The khalifah or successor to Muhammad ﷺ who organised the official version of the Qur'an.

 FOR INTEREST

Muslims believe that the Qur'an was revealed by Allah and sent down to earth through Jibril to the Prophet Muhammad ﷺ. It sets out rules and a way of living. Therefore, if human laws conflict with the Qur'an shouldn't Muslims feel free to ignore them since they must answer to a higher authority?

The Qur'an

The next two pages will help you to:

- explore the nature of the Qur'an
- explain the importance of the Qur'an
- evaluate the Qur'an as a source of authority for Muslims.

The Qur'an being read in a madrassah.

The Qur'an

The word **Qur'an** is Arabic and it means to 'recite'. Originally the Qur'an was memorised and repeated. However, Muhammad ﷺ also made special arrangements for it to be written down by people such as Zayd ibn Thabit and others.

The Mother of Books

Muslims call the Qur'an the Umm-ul-kitab or 'Mother of Books'. Muslims believe that it is the single most important book of the human race. The Qur'an is the actual word of Allah and to many it would be considered the nearest thing that there is to Allah in this world. Muhammad ﷺ did not write this book, he merely passed on and recited what Allah had told him.

AO1 skills **ACTIVITIES**

Can you name a book which has been life changing for either you or someone else? Why do you think Muslims describe the Qur'an as the 'Mother of Books'?

A belief exists in Islam that the Qur'an itself is eternal and the copy which exists on earth is a copy of the original in heaven. However, this belief suggests that all the other books given to the earlier prophets such as Ibrahim, Musa, Dawud and Isa were also copies of the Qur'an and it was only Muhammad ﷺ who received the entire Qur'an.

The language of the Qur'an

If a non-Muslim without knowledge of Arabic were to read, or listen to, the Qur'an there would be great difficulty in following the language and the meaning.

However if the listener could understand Arabic the reaction would be very different. In its original the Arabic flows in a beautiful form and many Muslims will experience an intense feeling from reading it. Muslims believe that Arabic is the language of Allah because it is the language in which the Qur'an was revealed. If the Qur'an is eternal so the language of Arabic must be the language of Allah.

The Qur'an is Allah's final message and its words can never be changed. As a result the Qur'an can only truly be read in Arabic since any translation will change the form and meaning of the words. Even if a Muslim does not speak Arabic they should learn it to read the Qur'an. The use of Arabic throughout Islam is a factor which unites the religion.

The Qur'an as a source of authority

A source of authority is something which has great power or meaning over the lives of individuals and communities. For Muslims the greatest possible source of authority on earth is the Qur'an since the words are those of Allah. The **Hadith** and **Sunnah** are also considered to be very important sources of authority in Islam but do not rival the Qur'an.

al-Fatihah

This is the first **Surah** or chapter of the Qur'an which is why it is called **al-Fatihah**, that is the Opening. It is also used as a prayer.

> **Surah 1**
>
> *With the Name of Allah, the Merciful Benefactor, The Merciful Redeemer*
> *In the name of Allah, Most Gracious, Most Merciful.*
> *Praise be to Allah, the Cherisher and Sustainer of the worlds;*
> *Most Gracious, Most Merciful;*
> *Master of the Day of Judgment.*
> *Thee do we worship, and Thine aid we seek.*
> *Show us the straight way,*
> *The way of those on whom Thou hast bestowed Thy Grace, those whose (portion)*
> *is not wrath, and who go not astray.*

ACTIVITIES

Read the words of al-Fatihah. What titles are used to describe Allah? Why do you think al-Fatihah was placed at the very beginning of the Qur'an? What does al-Fatihah say about Muslim beliefs about Allah?

The origins of the Qur'an

The cave of Hira on Mount Nur.

The Search

To understand the first human contact with the **Qur'an** it is necessary to go back to the year 610 CE to the cave of Hira on Mount Nur outside Makkah. It was here that a 40-year-old man named Muhammad ﷺ was about to have the answer to his spiritual search. Throughout his life Muhammad ﷺ had been searching for spiritual meaning, and tradition has it that he spent much of his time in prayer and solitude in the hills surrounding Makkah.

The Night of Power

Muhammad ﷺ was alone and praying in the cave of Hira on Mount Nur (sometimes called the Hill of Light). It was here that he had a very profound religious experience both for himself and the future development of Islam. In the darkness he heard a voice calling his name and a command to 'Recite'.

AO1 skills ACTIVITIES

Why is the Night of Power considered such an important event in the development of Islam? How did Muhammad ﷺ receive the words of the Qur'an? How were the words of the Qur'an passed on to the wider community?

An angel, Jibril the messenger of Allah, then appeared to Muhammad ﷺ. Jibril ordered Muhammad ﷺ to read the words. Jibril asked this three times but each time Muhammad ﷺ replied that he was unable to do so. This could either have been as a result of the fear which Muhammad ﷺ experienced during the encounter or, as popular tradition has it, he was unable to read or write. However, this being an encounter with Allah, Muhammad ﷺ experienced a rush of energy and suddenly these words stuck in his mind and he was able to repeat them aloud:

> **Surah 96:1–5**
> *Proclaim! (or read!) in the name of thy Lord and Cherisher, Who created –*
> *Created man, out of a (mere) clot of congealed blood:*
> *Proclaim! And thy Lord is Most Bountiful*
> *He Who taught (the use of) the pen*
> *Taught man that which he knew not.*

The experience ended as quickly as it started leaving a rather shocked Muhammad ﷺ to make his way home. This started the process of inspiring Muhammad ﷺ in his faith and he soon began gaining his first converts to Islam. This opening to **Surah** 96 was also the first revelation of the Qur'an to the human race.

Further revelations

Muhammad ﷺ did not receive the entire Qur'an in one go. Instead it was a lengthy and drawn out process which was to last over the next 23 years. His second revelation of Surah 74 did not happen until two years after the **Night of Power**.

During his lifetime Muhammad ﷺ experienced a number of revelations, some coming from Allah's messenger the angel Jibril and others coming direct from Allah. The nature of these experiences could vary and included some of the following characteristics.

- Muhammad ﷺ often went into hot, soaking sweats
- sometimes he would lose consciousness
- they could often happen in public places when he was speaking to others or doing something quite ordinary, like riding a horse
- others around him were often not aware that he was experiencing a revelation since it could often take only a matter of seconds
- some experiences occurred when Muhammad ﷺ was on his own
- Muhammad ﷺ describes some of his revelations like hearing a bell ringing
- in some cases the experience took him close to a feeling of death and a sensation that he was about to leave his own body.

As soon as he received the revelation of the next part of the Qu'ran he taught it to his close friends and followers. It was their duty to memorise the words and pass them on to others. In this way the revelation of the Qur'an was passed on to the growing Muslim community. The final part of the Qur'an was received just before his death in 632 CE.

ACTIVITIES

Why do you think the Qur'an was revealed over a period of 23 years instead of all in one go? 'How do people know that God is speaking to them, it could just be a case of an overactive imagination or mental illness'. What is your view on this? Consider the views and opinions of others.

The compilation of the Qur'an

The next two pages will help you to:

- understand and explain the way in which the parts of the Qur'an were brought together
- consider the way in which the Qur'an finally reached its present form.

Verses from the Qur'an.

Compilation of the Qur'an

Muhammad ﷺ received the **Qur'an** over a 23-year period. However, it was received as an oral tradition, that is, words were not actually written down but were memorised by the Muslim community. In many societies throughout history where literacy is not strong this was a way of preserving history, laws and traditions. As well as Muhammad ﷺ many others in the Muslim community also knew the words of the Qur'an off by heart (these individuals were called the **hafiz**).

AO1 skills **ACTIVITIES**

Why do you think many Muslims did not think it was important to write down an official version of the Qur'an during Muhammad's ﷺ lifetime? What problems emerged which eventually led to the official version of the Qur'an being put together? Can you explain three things about the organisation of the Qur'an?

Hafsa's Chest

Towards the end of his life, Muhammad ﷺ started to dictate various chapters or **Surahs** to some of his secretaries (tradition has it that the prophet could neither read or write). At this stage in history, paper did not exist and most writing occurred on very expensive materials such as parchment and vellum.

However, due to the shortage of these expensive materials other options such as date leaves, pieces of animal bone, leather and even pieces of white stone were used. Muhammad ﷺ checked these to ensure they were an accurate record and they were then handed over for safe keeping. No attempt was made to organise these writings in any way. It was felt at the time that the words of the Qur'an would be safe in the memories of the hafiz.

After the death of Muhammad ﷺ in 632 CE Islam began a rapid expansion into neighbouring regions. Many of the leaders of these Muslim armies were hafiz and battle deaths began to kill them off in large numbers. There was also the added problem that differences were beginning to appear in the hafiz memories of different parts of the Qur'an.

Muhammad's ﷺ close friend Abu Bakr gave orders that Muhammad's ﷺ chief personal secretary, Zaid ibn Thabit, make an accurate copy of the Qur'an. Zaid ibn Thabit used as his basis the written documents which were kept in Hafsa's wooden chest. However, no attempts were made to organise the chapters.

New developments

Although Abu Bakr started the process of collecting together the official Qur'an this did not go far enough. New problems began to emerge when the Qur'an was introduced into newly conquered non-Arabic parts of the Middle East.

New converts to Islam began to recite the Qur'an in their own regional dialects and accents which was having an impact on the way the Qur'an was recited. Imagine in today's world how English is spoken with many regional accents and the way that the language has developed. Despite the work of Zaid ibn Thabit it also seems that four different versions of the written Qur'an were in circulation.

The official Qur'an

The third khalifah was **Uthman**; he was determined to deal with this problem of the Qur'an. A meeting was ordered of all Muhammad's ﷺ secretaries and they looked through the contents of Hafsa's wooden chest to produce the official version of the Qur'an. Eventually the official version of the Qur'an was unveiled and all other versions were ordered to be destroyed. This whole process had taken many years to complete since the death of Muhammad ﷺ. All modern versions of the Qur'an are based on this official version.

ACTIVITIES

Could the Qur'an of today really be the original Qur'an? What is your view and what might the views of others be?

Why is the Qur'an so important to Muslims?

The next two pages will help you to:

- understand the way in which Allah had previously tried to bring humanity a message
- consider Muslim attitudes towards the interpretation of the Qur'an.

The Qur'an: the last revealed message to humanity

Muslims believe that before Muhammad ﷺ there were about 124,000 different prophets who were each given a message to reveal to humanity. However, of those prophets, four of them were important figures who also appear in Judaism and Christianity:

- Ibrahim (Abraham)
- Musa (Moses)
- Dawud (David)
- Isa (Jesus).

Each of these prophets was given a holy book of their own to reveal to humanity:

- Ibrahim was given a scroll called the Sahifa.
- Musa was given the Tawrah (Torah)
- Dawud was given the Zabur (Psalms)
- Isa was given the Injil (Gospels).

However, Muslims believe that these books and revelations were not looked after properly. The Sahifah, Tawrah, Zabur and Injil were changed in various ways with additions made and bits left out, for example the Injil was changed to say that Isa (Jesus) was Allah's son and not just a prophet. Although these books are still used by Jews and Christians, Muslims feel that the messages in them are unreliable and therefore should be discounted:

ACTIVITIES

What were the problems with the earlier revelations for Muslims before the Qur'an? Why is the Qur'an so important to Muslims? Why do many Muslims believe that the Qur'an is unchangeable?

> **Surah 6:91**
>
> *No just estimate of Allah do they make when they say: 'Nothing doth Allah send down to man (by way of revelation)'. Say: 'Who then sent down the Book which Moses brought – a light and guidance to man: But ye make it into (separate) sheets for show, while ye conceal much (of its contents): therein were ye taught that which ye knew not – neither ye nor your fathers.' Say: 'Allah (sent it down)': Then leave them to plunge in vain discourse and trifling.*

Allah has therefore revealed one final and complete message to humanity.

Why is the Qur'an so important to Muslims?

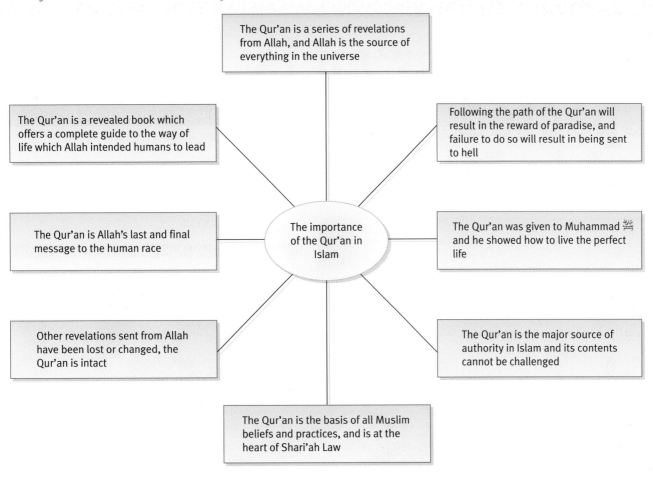

The Qur'an is a series of revelations from Allah, and Allah is the source of everything in the universe

The Qur'an is a revealed book which offers a complete guide to the way of life which Allah intended humans to lead

Following the path of the Qur'an will result in the reward of paradise, and failure to do so will result in being sent to hell

The Qur'an is Allah's last and final message to the human race

The importance of the Qur'an in Islam

The Qur'an was given to Muhammad ﷺ and he showed how to live the perfect life

Other revelations sent from Allah have been lost or changed, the Qur'an is intact

The Qur'an is the major source of authority in Islam and its contents cannot be challenged

The Qur'an is the basis of all Muslim beliefs and practices, and is at the heart of Shari'ah Law

Surah 2:2

This is the Book; in it is guidance sure, without doubt, to those who fear Allah.

Interpretation of the Qur'an

The **Qur'an** is the word of Allah and cannot be challenged, it is infallible. However understanding what the Qur'an says is a complex matter:

- Meanings are not always clear since passages from one part of the book need to be used to explain another part. Only a detailed linking of these passages will allow the reader to make links.
- Parts of the Qur'an were explained by Muhammad ﷺ through the **Hadith** and the **Sunnah**.
- Some of the interpretations of the Qur'an by those close to Muhammad ﷺ were also seen as acceptable.
- In Shi'ah Islam the Imams are allowed to interpret the Qur'an.

ACTIVITIES

What could be the problems of having a holy book which no one is allowed to challenge? Surah 5 was the last part of the revelation of the Qur'an given to Muhammad ﷺ. In Surah 5 verse 3 Allah states: 'This day have I perfected your religion for you, completed My favour upon you, and have chosen for you Islam as your religion.' What do you think this means?

How the Qur'an is respected and used in Islam

The next two pages will help you to:

- understand how and why the Qur'an is shown respect
- explain what is meant by a hafiz
- evaluate the use of the Qur'an in public and private worship.

The Qur'an mounted on a stand, or kursi.

The **Qur'an** is a unique book, it is something which Allah revealed to humanity and it is seen as His final message. For that reason the Qur'an must be treated with the greatest care and respect.

How is respect shown to the Qur'an?

In the Muslim community many practical steps can be taken to show respect towards the Qur'an. These would include:

- purity is required (being in a state of wudu)
- to read it a person must be in the right frame of mind and must concentrate on it

AO1 skills **ACTIVITIES**

Can you think of something precious which would be of tremendous value to you? How would you treat such a precious object?

- people should not speak whilst it is being read
- eating and drinking around the Qur'an may be considered disrespectful
- unnecessary noise should not be made around the Qur'an such as music playing
- a woman must not touch it whilst she is having her period
- the Qur'an should be protected from dirt and dust
- when not in use it should be positioned so that nothing is placed on or above it
- the Qur'an should not touch the ground – to prevent this it is often placed on a special stool called a kursi
- if possible the reader should face the direction of Makkah.

 **RESEARCH NOTE**

What part does the Qur'an play in public and private worship in Islam?

The hafiz

The greatest honour which can be paid to the Qur'an is for someone to memorise it word perfect from beginning to end. There are thousands of such people in Islam and they are given an honorary title of **hafiz** and great acclaim in society. It is believed that someone who becomes a hafiz will be rewarded with a place in heaven.

Calligraphy

Islam forbids the use of human, or even animal, forms in places of worship and in decorating the Qur'an. As a result the art of **calligraphy** (or beautiful writing) grew up as a way of honouring and decorating copies of the Qur'an. The act of producing the calligraphy in its many beautiful forms is an act of worship in its own right.

How is the Qur'an used in public worship?

The Qur'an is central to Muslim belief and it is only natural to expect it to be used in worship. There are public readings of the Qur'an at the Friday Jumu'ah prayers and an imam will make reference to it in his sermon or khutbah.

During the month of Ramadan there are public readings of the Qur'an. The Qur'an is divided into thirty equal parts called juz and these are read over the course of the month.

The Qur'an is also read at special events such as marriages and funerals. At a marriage ceremony it is popular to read from **Surah** 4 (the Woman) which has a special meaning for couples.

How is the Qur'an used in private worship?

For many Muslims, reading the Qur'an on their own or with a small group of others will form an important part of private worship. The Qur'an could be opened at random and that particular part of the book could be read or it could be a more systematic reading of the text each day. Many Muslims will attempt to memorise parts of the text which they feel are important to them. Parts of the Qur'an can be meditated upon and the worshipper will feel it to be a source of inspiration.

The organisation of the Qur'an

The organisation of the Qur'an

The **Qur'an** is not a book with a beginning, middle and end but is instead a collection of revelations from Allah. The Qur'an is organised and structured in the following way:

- the Qur'an contains 114 chapters called **Surahs**
- with the exception of Surah 1 all the Surahs are organised by length with Surah 2 being the longest and Surah 108 being the shortest

The next two pages will help you to:

- understand the contents of the Qur'an
- explain how the Surahs of the Qur'an are organised.

The al-Fatihah.

Sūra I.

Fātiha, or The Opening Chapter.

1. *In the name of Allah, Most Gracious, Most Merciful.*

2. Praise be to Allah,
    The Cherisher and Sustainer of the Worlds ;

3. Most Gracious, Most Merciful ;

4. Master of the Day of Judgment.

5. Thee do we worship,
    And thine aid we seek.

6. Show us the straight way ;

7. The way of those on whom
    Thou hast bestowed Thy Grace,
    Those whose (portion)
    Is not wrath,
    And who go not astray.

- the first Surah, called **al-Fatihah** (The Opening), is different to the other Surahs and takes the form of a short prayer

- each Surah is given a name which is based upon a prominent word which appears in that chapter but sometimes has nothing to do with its contents, for example Surah 2 is called The Cow, Surah 6 is The Cattle, Surah 16 is The Bee and Surah 17 is The Night Journey

- with the exception of Surah 9 all the chapters open with Bismillah 'With the Name of Allah, the Merciful Benefactor, The Merciful Redeemer'. This is to show that the Qur'an originates with Allah

- each Surah is subdivided into verses called ayat: the longest Surah has 286 verses (Surah 2) and the shortest has only 3 verses (Surah 108 'Abundance')

With the Name of Allah, the Merciful Benefactor, The Merciful Redeemer To thee have We granted the Fount (of Abundance). Therefore to thy Lord turn in Prayer and Sacrifice. For he who hateth thee, he will be cut off (from Future Hope).

- the Surahs are also divided into the Makkan and Madinan revelations. This sometimes depends on where Muhammad ﷺ was when he received them. The Makkan Surahs are accepted by experts as being the earliest and can generally be recognised as they have shorter verses. The Makkan Surahs are mostly concentrated near the end of the Qur'an.

- The first copies of the Qur'an were written in kufic script and usually on vellum.

- Arabic is written only using consonants so in the 10th century CE vowel signs were added to the Qur'an to help people with pronunciation. However, although there are different accepted ways of reading the Qur'an there are no variant texts such as are found in the holy books of some other religions.

ACTIVITIES

'All sacred books should be translated into modern language so that people can understand them more easily.' What is your opinion? What do you think a Muslim would say?

The contents of the Qur'an (1)

Key beliefs within the Qur'an

Within the text of the **Qur'an** are found the essential key beliefs of Islam. The key beliefs within the Qur'an can be summarised as follows:

There is only One God – Allah

> **Surah 112**
>
> *Allah is absolute or alone, He has no equals or rivals and is eternal. He is omnipotent and is the creator of everything in the universe. Humans must surrender to the will of Allah:*
>
> *Say: He is Allah, the One and Only;*
> *Allah, the Eternal, Absolute;*
> *He begetteth not, nor is He begotten;*
> *And there is none like unto Him.*

> **Surah 2:255**
>
> *Allah! There is no god but He – the Living, the Self-subsisting, Eternal. No slumber can seize Him nor sleep. His are all things in the heavens and on earth. Who is there can intercede in His presence except as He permitteth? He knoweth what (appeareth to His creatures as) before or after or behind them. Nor shall they compass aught of His knowledge except as He willeth. His Throne doth extend over the heavens and the earth, and He feeleth no fatigue in guarding and preserving them for He is the Most High, the Supreme (in glory).*

Angels are recognised as the servants of Allah

> **Surah 82:10–12**
>
> *But verily over you (are appointed angels) to protect you –*
> *Kind and honourable – Writing down (your deeds):*
> *They know (and understand) all that ye do.*

The next two pages will help you to:

- understand which key beliefs of Islam are found in the Qur'an
- explain some of the key beliefs.

AO1 skills — ACTIVITIES

What key Muslim beliefs come from the Qur'an? Why is it important to use the original text of the Qur'an to inform these key beliefs?

RESEARCH NOTE

Look up the following verses in the Qur'an and write them down: Surah 47:19, 14:35, 2:224, 62:9, 17:23, 5:32, 17:32, 5:38, 2:283, 20:131. You will need these for the activity at the end of this lesson.

Other types of spiritual beings called Jinn also exist in a parallel spiritual world. These spirits or Jinn can be good or bad and Shaytan (or Iblis) is one of them. Shaytan is active in the world trying to tempt Muslims away from the path that Allah has created for them:

> **Surah 15:28–315**
>
> *Behold! Thy Lord said to the angels: 'I am about to create man, from sounding clay from mud moulded into shape;*
> *When I have fashioned him (in due proportion) and breathed into him of My spirit, fall ye down in obeisance unto him.'*
> *So the angels prostrated themselves, all of them together:*
> *Not so Iblis: he refused to be among those who prostrated themselves.*

The Qur'an warns about the Day of Judgement and life after death

Humans must prepare themselves for this event and its consequences. There will be no second chance:

> **Surah 23:99–100**
>
> *(In Falsehood will they be) Until, when death comes to one of them, he says:*
> *'O my Lord! Send me back (to life) –*
> *In order that I may work righteousness in the things I neglected.' – 'By no means! It is but a word he says.' – Before them is a Partition till the Day they are raised up.*

The Role of Muhammad ﷺ

Muhammad ﷺ is seen as the messenger of Allah and he brought Allah's final message to humanity:

> **Surah 3:144**
>
> *Muhammad is no more than an apostle: many Were the apostle that passed away before him. If he died or were slain, will ye then Turn back on your heels? If any did turn back on his heels, not the least harm will he do to Allah; but Allah (on the other hand) will swiftly reward those who (serve Him) with gratitude.*

ACTIVITIES

Why do you think that sacred texts are so important in a religion? Earlier you researched ten passages from the Qur'an. Why do you think these rules are so important that they should be included in a holy book? Look at the passages from the Qur'an that you copied: are there any of these rules which might apply to a non-Muslim? Are such rules still relevant to modern 21st-century living?

The contents of the Qur'an (2)

As well as forming the basis of belief in Islam the **Qur'an** is also a source from which an acceptable way of life is drawn. The Qur'an has a great influence on how Islam is actually practised in the modern world.

Salah

Regular Salah (or prayer) is a key feature of being a Muslim. The Qur'an tells Muslims:

> ### Surah 4:103
>
> *When ye pass (Congregational) prayers, celebrate Allah's praises, standing, sitting down, or lying down on your sides; but when ye are free from danger, set up Regular Prayers: For such prayers are enjoined on believers at stated times.*

The actual timings of the prayers are not specified in the Qur'an and Muslims had to look to Muhammad ﷺ on this matter. However, the Qur'an does give guidance on how to pray.

During prayer a Muslim will begin by reciting Surah 1 of the Qur'an, **al-Fatihah**.

Friday or Jumu'ah prayer was also set by the Qur'an:

> ### Surah 62:10
>
> *And when the Prayer is finished, then may ye disperse through the land, and seek of the Bounty of Allah: and celebrate the Praises of Allah often (and without stint): that ye may prosper.*

Zakah

Another Pillar of Islam is zakah, the purification of wealth by payment of annual welfare due. Again the key religious practice is based on instructions from the Qur'an:

> ### Surah 2:110
>
> *And be steadfast in prayer and regular in charity: And whatever good ye send forth for your souls before you, ye shall find it with Allah: for Allah sees Well all that ye do*

The problem which the Qur'an does present for Muslims here is that it does not specify at how much zakah should actually have been set. This problem was dealt with by Muhammad ﷺ.

The next two pages will help you to:

- understand more of the key beliefs of Islam found in the Qur'an
- explain what the Qur'an teaches about the Five Pillars of Islam
- consider the importance of these beliefs in Muslim life.

AO1 skills **ACTIVITIES**

Write down some ideas of how the Qu'ran influences the practice of Islam in the modern world. Discuss with a partner.

> ### Surah 2:43
>
> *And be steadfast in prayer; practise regular charity; and bow down your heads with those who bow down (in worship).*

Zakah applies to crops and animals as well as money.

Prayer at Ramadan.

Fasting

The Qur'an is also central here on specifying that fasting should be practised by Muslims.

From this and other statements in the Qur'an grew the Muslim practice of fasting during the month of Ramadan.

Pilgrimage – Hajj

The Hajj, the pilgrimage to Makkah, one of the Five Pillars of Islam, must be performed at least once in a lifetime (if a person is able to do so). Surah 22 (verses 26–38) gives detail on how the Hajj is to be performed but the timetable of events is not given. Instead Muslims have to look to the example of Muhammad ﷺ in the **Hadith** on what should be done here.

Food and alcohol

The Qur'an impacts on the daily lives of many Muslims perhaps in a way the holy books of other religions may not. Islam has a number of food laws which are based on the text of the Qur'an. Most foods are permitted but there are some restrictions (see Surah 2:172–173).

The Qur'an forbids the eating of pork (or any of the variations it might appear in such as bacon or ham), eating the blood of any animal, eating an animal which has died of natural causes or has been killed other than in the name of Allah.

Alcohol is also banned in a Muslim society because the Qur'an expressively forbids it:

> **Surah 5:90**
>
> *O ye who believe! Intoxicants and gambling, (dedication of) stones, and (divination by) arrows, are an abomination – of Satan's handwork: eschew such (abomination), that ye may prosper.*

Economic life

The Qur'an forbids the lending or borrowing of money for interest (this is called riba or usury). This could have a major impact on life in the modern world because it makes it difficult for Muslims to have a mortgage, take out a loan to pay for an item such as a car and run up a credit card debt, and receive interest on savings.

The Qur'an also forbids any form of gambling which extends itself to placing bets, games of chance, buying lottery tickets and participating in raffles.

> **Surah 2:183–184**
>
> *O ye who believe! Fasting is prescribed to you as it was prescribed to those before you, that ye may (learn) self-restraint – (Fasting) for a fixed number of days; but if any of you is ill, or on a journey, the prescribed number (Should be made up) from days later. For those who can do it (With hardship), is a ransom, the feeding of one that is indigent. But he that will give more, of his own free will – it is better for him. And it is better for you that ye fast, if ye only knew.*

AO1 skills **ACTIVITIES**

What is the link between how Muslims practise their religion and the Qur'an? How far can it be said that the Qur'an, the revelations from Allah, has a major impact on the daily lives of Muslims?

> **Surah 2:172–173**
>
> *O ye who believe! Eat of the good things that We have provided for you, and be grateful to Allah, if it is Him ye worship. He hath only forbidden you dead meat, and blood, and the flesh of swine, and that on which any other name hath been invoked besides that of Allah. But if one is forced by necessity, without wilful disobedience, nor transgressing due limits – then is he guiltless. For Allah is Oft-forgiving Most Merciful.*

> **Surah 2:275**
>
> *Those who devour usury will not stand except as stand one whom the Evil one by his touch Hath driven to madness. That is because they say: 'Trade is like usury,' but Allah hath permitted trade and forbidden usury. Those who after receiving direction from their Lord, desist, shall be pardoned for the past; their case is for Allah (to judge); but those who repeat (The offence) are companions of the Fire: They will abide therein (for ever).*

The nature of the Hadith and Sunnah

The next two pages will help you to:

- understand the importance of the Hadith and Sunnah to Muslims
- explain how the Hadith were collected together.

The nature of the Hadith and Sunnah

Muhammad ﷺ was Allah's chosen messenger and to most in the Muslim world he was the final messenger. Therefore Muhammad ﷺ is seen as an example of the 'perfect man' or the 'model Muslim'.

As a result Muslims study closely every detail of Muhammad's ﷺ life no matter how insignificant or trivial. If Muhammad ﷺ did or said something then it is only right for others to follow his example. If the **Qur'an** is not always clear or does not mention something on a particular issue then to Muslims it seems logical to refer to the **Hadith** and the **Sunnah**.

The Hadith

The Hadith is a text of the recorded words, actions and instructions of the Prophet Muhammad ﷺ. Muslims use the Hadith when the Qur'an is not clear on a matter or perhaps does not say anything about it.

The problem of the Hadith

The problem with the Hadith is whether they were actually said by Muhammad ﷺ or not. Nearly three hundred years after the Prophet Muhammad's ﷺ death a Muslim scholar named Muhammad ibn Ismail made a collection of all the known Hadiths of Muhammad ﷺ and drew up a list of an incredible 600,000 Hadiths. Many of these Hadith had been passed on orally and as a result they may have been altered over time.

It was clear that many of these sayings were not genuine and some even contradicted the teachings of the Qur'an. So Muhammad ibn Ismail checked hundreds of thousands of Hadith and decided that unless they could be checked and traced back to the early followers and companions of Muhammad ﷺ they could not be considered as genuine.

As a result the total number of Hadith was reduced to 2,762. These Hadith became known as the **Sahih al-Bukhari**. However, many other collections of Hadith exist within the Muslim world. Some use the same principles which Bukhari applied and others do not. Shi'ah Muslims also have their own **Hadith of Ali** based on the sayings of the Prophet Muhammad's ﷺ cousin.

ACTIVITIES

Explain what is meant by the Hadith. Why are Hadith Qudsi considered to be the most important of the Hadiths?

Hadith Qudsi

The **Hadith Qudsi**, or Sacred Hadith, are so called because although Muhammad ﷺ spoke them, the meaning is from Allah expressed by Muhammad ﷺ. Their authority comes directly from Allah and not Muhammad ﷺ. The content of these Hadith tends to be about aspects of belief, worship and general conduct. See the sacred text box for examples of Hadith.

> **Hadith Qudsi**
>
> *If he has in his heart goodness to the weight of one barley corn, and has said there is no God but Me, he shall come out of hell-fire.*

> **Hadith Al-Daraqutni**
>
> *Do not harm yourselves or others.*

The Sunnah

The word Sunnah means 'path' or 'beaten track'. It is a collection of actions and examples from the life of Muhammad ﷺ which are contained within the Hadith. An example from the Qur'an tells Muslims to pray:

> **Surah 4:103**
>
> *When ye pass (Congregational) prayers, celebrate Allah's praises, standing, sitting down, or lying down on your sides; but when ye are free from danger, set up Regular Prayers: For such prayers are enjoined on believers at stated times.*

However, it does not tell Muslims how to pray. Instead Muslims must refer to the Sunnah or how Muhammad ﷺ actually showed Muslims to prepare for and perform prayer. The same could also be said for paying zakah, performing fasting during Ramadan and completing the pilgrimage to Makkah.

ACTIVITIES

Can the addition of sacred texts, other than the Qur'an, help or hinder a Muslim today? 'The only sacred text in Islam should be the Qur'an since all others are unreliable.' What is your view and the view of others on this matter?

Sacred writings in Islam: a summary

The next two pages will help you to:

- summarise the most important beliefs and teachings about sacred writings in Islam
- explain the importance of the Qur'an, Hadith and Sunnah
- consider the relative importance of the Muslim sacred texts.

Sacred writings in Islam

There are three sacred texts in Islam:

- the **Qur'an** which is the most important
- the **Hadith** which are Muhammad's ﷺ words
- the **Sunnah** which are the actions of Muhammad ﷺ.

The Qur'an

The key facts of the Qu'ran can be summarised as listed below.

- The Qu'ran contains the actual words of Allah as received by Muhammad ﷺ.
- It is the final message to the human race; all other messages were distorted.
- The Qur'an is eternal and the original exists in heaven.
- The Prophet Muhammad ﷺ received the Qur'an through a series of revelations beginning with the **Night of Power**.
- Originally the book was memorised by the Muslim community and new parts were taught as they were revealed.
- The revelation of the Qur'an took nearly 23 years to complete.
- Early in its history Muhammad ﷺ had the Qur'an written down but there was no structure or organisation to the arrangement of the **Surahs**.
- After the death of Muhammad ﷺ concerns were were raised about the Qur'an as memories began to fade.
- In 652 CE the khalifah **Uthman** unveiled the official version of the Qur'an. All others were destroyed and all modern copies date back to this.

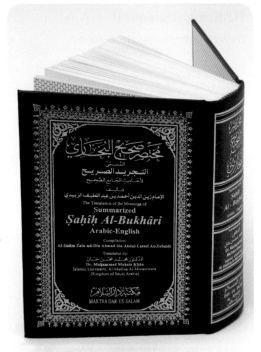

Hadith Sahih al-Bukhari.

The structure of the Qur'an

- The Qur'an is organised in 114 separate chapters called Surahs.
- The Surahs are organised from longest (Surah 2) to shortest (Surah 108).
- Each Surah is given a distinctive name.
- Surah 1 is **al-Fatihah** or opening prayer which is used at Salah.
- The language of the Qur'an is Arabic which is believed to be the language of Allah.
- The quality of the written Arabic is very high and its form can move those who listen to or read it.

The contents of the Qur'an

- The Qur'an is central to Muslim belief and practices.
- It explains the nature of Allah who is all powerful, eternal and without equal.
- The book sets out the path which Allah intends humans to follow and details the rewards and punishments of the afterlife and the dangers of Shaytan.
- The Qur'an is also the basis of many of the practices of Islam, although Muslims often need to turn to the Hadith for greater detail and explanation.
- Matters covered in the Qur'an include prayer, fasting, giving to charity, the Hajj, marriage, food laws, gambling, usury, dress, sexual behavior and general rules for community living.

The Hadith

- An important secondary religious text in Islam.
- A collection of the sayings of the Prophet Muhammad ﷺ.
- This text is often used when the Qur'an does not give sufficient detail or explanation, or when the Qur'an says nothing about an issue.
- The most reliable Hadith are found in the **Hadith of Bukhari** but other collections do exist.
- The **Hadith Qudsi** are considered the most sacred Hadith since they are believed to be further revelations from Allah to the Prophet rather than just the Prophet's own words.
- Both Shi'ah and Sunni Muslims also use the **Hadith of Ali**.

The Sunnah

- The word Sunnah means 'path' or 'beaten track'.
- The Sunnah are a collection of examples from the life of Muhammad ﷺ which are found in the Hadith.
- The Sunnah are used to help a Muslim understand in greater detail when something is unclear in the Qur'an. For example the Qur'an states that Hajj needs to be performed but does not give details of the structure of the pilgrimage. The example set by Muhammad ﷺ in the Sunnah is used.

The use and treatment of the Qur'an in Islam

- The Qur'an is the word of Allah and it must be treated with the greatest of respect at all times.
- Such respect is shown by touching it only when in a state of purity or touching it with something other than bare hands, not placing it upon the floor, it has to be the highest placed book, no eating or drinking whilst reading it.
- The words of the Qur'an are sacred and infallible (cannot be challenged).
- Special forms of writing were developed to express the beauty of the text. This is called calligraphy.
- Muslims who have memorised the entire text of the Qur'an are known as **Hafiz**.
- In public worship there are readings of the Qur'an; it is used as the basis of the sermon or Khutbah delivered at the Friday or Jumu'ah prayer. Extracts from the Qur'an, particularly Surah 1, al-Fatihah, are recited during Salah.
- In private worship the Qur'an is read and also recited during Salah.

Welcome to the Grade Studio

GCSE is about what you can do, not what you can't do. You need to know what examiners want in your answers so you can get the best possible marks. In GCSE Religious Studies there are two things that examiners are looking for. These are called assessment objectives (AO). Questions are designed to help examiners find out how well you do in each assessment objective.

Graded examples for this topic

AO1

AO1 questions test what you know and how well you can explain and analyse things. Let's look at an AO1 question to see what examiners expect you to do.

Question

Why is the Qur'an so important to Muslims?   **[6 marks]**

Such a question will be measured by the examiner in levels of response. The more detailed and relevant the answer the greater the level, and more importantly, the mark. **Remember the exam is about maximising your mark potential.**

Student's answer

I think the Qur'an is important to Islams because it is an important book. It was given to them by god 100s of years ago in a cave. The book is so important that they don't eat or drink around it and it tells them what they must do.

Examiner's comment

This is a weak *Level 1* answer. There is little in the way of relevant information. Some credit could be given for the fact that the Qur'an is important in Islam because it comes from Allah but little attempt has been made to develop this. This student also fails to use specialist terms referring to Muslims as 'Islams' and 'god' instead of Allah. To reach a *Level 2* the student would need to offer more relevant information in a structured form with relevant specialist terms.

Student's improved answer

The Qur'an is important to Muslims because it is a book revealed to Muhammad (PBUH) by Allah. The Qur'an was given in a series of visions lasting twenty three years. This book is an authority for Muslims and tells them everything they need to know.

Examiner's comment

This has now risen to a satisfactory answer. The student has offered relevant information (which is still lacking in detail) in a structured and organised way. Better use has been made of specialist words.

Student's improved answer

The Qur'an is important to Muslims because it is Allah's final message to the human race. All previous scriptures given by Allah to the human race have been lost or changed therefore it is important to keep this one intact. The words of the Qur'an are considered to be the actual words of Allah as given to the Prophet Muhammad (PBUH) in a series of revelations. The Qur'an offers guidance on what a Muslim must believe and practise in order to be rewarded by a place in heaven.

Examiner's comment

A very detailed and complete answer full of relevant information and explanation. The answer is well structured and easy to follow. Very good use has been made of key specialist terms. *Level 3.*

Question

Sacred writings are more important than religious leaders. Discuss this statement. You should include different, supported points of view and a personal viewpoint.   **[12 marks]**

This question is trying to test your ability to present more than one point of view and to evaluate them. The quality of your answer will be graded in levels, the better the answer the higher the level. A weak answer is often just a personal viewpoint with very little supporting evidence or argument and will often be one-sided. A very good answer will draw on a range of different viewpoints, use relevant evidence and argument and will be written in a very clear, easy-to-follow way.

Level 1

The candidate will demonstrate little understanding of the question. The answer will be too simple with little or no relevant information.

First show the examiner that you understand what the question is about and then state an opinion. For example, the Qur'an is more important than a leader because it comes from Allah.

Level 2

The candidate will show a little understanding of the question. Some relevant information will be included but often the answer is one-sided.

Next go on to justify this point of view by referring to religious belief. For example, Muslims believe that the Qur'an is the actual word of Allah, religious leaders are not as important.

Level 3

The candidate will show a satisfactory understanding of the question with a range of relevant material and appropriate evidence.

For the next stage offer a deeper explanation. The Qur'an is Allah's final and complete word to the human race. Many Muslims have to learn Arabic to read the Qur'an. The Qur'an offers a Muslim complete guidance on how to live a Muslim way of life. Offer a different viewpoint. For example, you might wish to include the fact that the Qur'an is not always clear and a leader such as Muhammad ﷺ is needed to interpret the holy books. You should also offer your own opinion.

Level 4

The candidate will show a clear understanding of the question with a range of fully supported viewpoints backed by relevant evidence and argument.

Finally offer a deeper explanation of both viewpoints. You might mention that amongst Shi'ah Muslims some Imams have the power to interpret the Qur'an. The Prophet also offered interpretations through the Hadith.

You might like to counter this argument by saying that the Qur'an has remained constant for nearly 1400 years. Leaders come and go but the Qur'an is eternal.

Finally, you need to offer your own opinion and explain why you think as you do.

These specimen answers provide an outline of how you could construct your response. Space does not allow us to give a full response. The examiner will be looking for more detail in your actual exam responses.

Remember and Reflect

AO1 Describe, explain and analyse, using knowledge and understanding

Find the answer on:

1 Explain in one sentence what each of the following are.
a Qur'an
b Hadith
c Sunnah
d calligraphy
e hafiz
f Night of Power.

PAGE 145

2 Why was the Night of Power such a significant event in the revelation of the Qur'an?

PAGE 148–149

3 How was the Qur'an revealed to the Prophet Muhammad ﷺ?

PAGE 148–149

4 Explain why the Qur'an needed to be written into a book form.

PAGE 150–151

5 List five reasons why the Qur'an is so important to Muslims.

PAGE 153

6 How is the Qur'an organised?

PAGE 164

7 Explain how the Qur'an is used in:
a public worship
b private worship.

PAGE 155

8 How does the Muslim community show respect towards the Qur'an?

PAGE 154–155

9 Explain what the Hadith are.

PAGE 162–163

10 How are the Hadith used.

PAGE 162

11 What is the Sunnah and how is it used?

PAGE 163

12 Explain the importance of Arabic and calligraphy in modern copies of the Qur'an.

PAGE 164–165

AO2 Use evidence and reasoned argument to express and evaluate personal responses, informed insights, and differing viewpoints

1 Can the words of the Qur'an be trusted? Give reasons for your views.

2 Do you think that holy books are all people need to understand God? What is your view? Why?

3 'It isn't important what is in holy books; it is what religious people do.' Explain your own views in relation to this statement and the views of others.

4 'Every religion needs a holy book to guide its followers.' Explain your own view and those of others.

Your view	Muslim view	Another view

exam Café

Welcome

Welcome to Exam Café. Here you can get ready for your exam through a range of revision tools and exam preparation activities designed to help you get the most out of your revision time.

Tools and tips

Now you have finished the course/unit, it is time to revise and prepare for the examination.

A key to any exam is the revision and preparation leading up to it. The key to good revision is to 'work smart'. This section will guide you to know what is needed for success and, just as important, what is not. So don't panic! Think positive, because the examiner will. GCSE is about what you can do, not what you cannot.

Key points to note at this stage

There are two important points to consider before you begin your revision programme:

1 Your revision will need to focus on what the examiner is looking for in the answers so that you can achieve the best possible mark. Remember that the examiners are looking for the AO1 and AO2 assessment objectives. Each of these objectives is worth 50 per cent of the total mark.

2 You also need to know that the exam questions on the paper are designed to test your performance with both AO1 and AO2 objectives. Each question will be made up of five parts:

   a Four AO1 parts, of which three check your knowledge and one tests your understanding and analysis.

   b One question testing AO2 – your ability to consider different points of view on a particular issue and how much you can express your own points of view with relevant evidence and argument.

Now you understand what the examiner is looking for, it is necessary to turn to your revision programme.

How to get started

An important key to success with any exam is the preparation beforehand. While few people enjoy the process of revision, it is vital for success. Your class teacher will also discuss revision with you. Below are some suggestions and ideas that can be employed:

1 It is vital to revise in plenty of time before the exam. Do not leave everything to the last minute.

2 Design a revision timetable and be realistic about what can be achieved.

3 Revision is a personal matter and we all learn in different ways. Remember that many revision skills can be transferred between different subjects.

4 These are some suggested revision techniques:

- Create summary cards for each topic – a maximum of five-to-ten bullet points on each card.

- Create lists of key words and terms. Ask somebody to test you on them or hang them around the house.

- Create a mind map to summarise a major topic.

- Design cards with a word or idea on one side and a question/ definition or answer on the other. These allow you to be tested by family members or friends who may not have much subject knowledge.

- Create an A–Z list on a certain topic. This involves writing the twenty-six letters of the alphabet down the side of a page and then having to write a key word or teaching connected to that topic for each letter of the alphabet.

- Remember that religious teachings do not have to be learnt word-for-word. It is acceptable to paraphrase them.

5 Break your revision into sessions of 5–10 minutes to start with (this can be increased as you become much better at it). Give yourself a short break (of about 5 minutes) and then go back to revising. Remember that sitting there and revising when nothing is going in is as bad as doing no revision at all.

6 Try answering questions on past papers then marking them with the mark scheme yourself. Alternatively, you can write your own questions and develop your own mark scheme. Answer the questions and use the levels of response to mark them.

7 Finally, remember that if you go into revision with a negative attitude you are ultimately going to make it much tougher on yourself.

ExamCafé

Revision
Common errors and mistakes

So the day of the exam has arrived. Remember that you are not the first to sit exams and you will not be the last. However, learn from the experience of others and do not fall into any of the following exam traps:

Misreading the question

Take a minute and READ the question carefully. A surprisingly large number of candidates do not read the questions carefully. They simply see a word or miss a point and feel they have to start writing. No matter how good your answer is, if it does not answer the question it will not gain you any marks.

Wasting valuable time

The exam is a race against the clock. Match the length of your response to the number of marks being awarded. A 1-mark question can be answered with a sentence and not a paragraph.

Poor selection of knowledge

Choose good examples that help you to develop and explain your ideas. For example, if a question asks you to explain why it is important for Muslims to read the Qur'an, don't just answer 'because their religion requires it'.

Disorganised waffle

Written answers, especially AO2-style answers, require you to plan your answer thoughtfully. It requires a range of viewpoints, including religious responses and your own views. Be careful and do not let your own views take over.

Know the exam paper

Make sure that you fully understand the layout and instructions for the exam paper. In particular focus on which questions you must do and how many questions you are required to do.

It is Religious Studies after all

Remember that the subject is Religious Studies and you will be tested on your knowledge and understanding of religion and its impact on the lives of individuals and communities. Make sure your answers contain relevant religious ideas.

Revision check list

The details of the course are known as the Specification. It is broken down into the units listed below. There is a summary of the key areas within each unit that you need to know about.

TOPIC 1 CORE BELIEFS

- know the meaning of all key words so you can answer a factual question, for example: 'What is meant by a prophet?'
- know and understand the importance of each belief for Muslims and how it affects their lifestyle, for example understanding the Day of Judgement
- know and understand how topics connect, for example Allah, the Prophets and the Day of Judgement are all connected.

TOPIC 2 SPECIAL DAYS AND PILGRIMAGE

- know how Muslims celebrate special days and why they are important
- know in detail about Hajj and what Muslims do on Hajj
- know and understand how festivals can help believers, for example by deepening personal faith or educating children about their religion.

TOPIC 3 MAJOR DIVISIONS AND INTERPRETATIONS

- focus on differences in worship, belief, organisation and the practices of Sunni, Shi'ah and Sufi Muslims
- understand how the differences came about between the divisions
- understand how Islam is practised in the UK and other parts of the world.

TOPIC 4 PLACES AND FORMS OF WORSHIP

- demonstrate a detailed knowledge of a mosque
- understand the acts of public and private worship in Islam
- understand the role of religious leaders
- understand the importance of worship to a believer.

TOPIC 5 RELIGION IN THE FAITH COMMUNITY AND THE FAMILY

- understand what happens at rites of passage ceremonies
- understand the Ummah and the Islamic way of life
- understand the importance of the family in Islam and the role of men and women.

TOPIC 6 SACRED WRITINGS

- know the nature and organisation of the Qur'an and the Sunnah (Ahadith)
- display a knowledge and understanding of how sacred writings are used in Islam
- know the importance of the Qur'an in Islam

ExamCafé

Exam preparation
Sample student answers

Now you have done some serious revision, it is time to see what sort of response to the questions will get good marks in the exam. Here are some examples of responses with comments from the examiner to show you what is good about them and how they could be improved. Remember examiners will use levels of response for part d) which is AO1 and part e) which is AO2. For parts a), b) and c) responses will be point marked. This means that if there is 1 mark allocated for the question, only one point is expected, if two marks are allocated, then two points are expected and so on. Part a) is worth 1 mark, b) 2 marks and c) 3 marks.

AO1

Here are some AO1 point-marked questions and example responses from Unit 1 Core beliefs.

State the Muslim name for God. **[1 mark]**

Allah.

Examiner Tip
'State' is examiner speak for 'name' or 'give'.

Examiner says
This answer could be given as a single word or a short sentence. Further explanation is not needed.

How do Muslims show their beliefs about Allah? **[3 marks]**

Muslims follow the teachings of the Qur'an which are Allah's actual words. Muslims worship directly to Allah, since it is to him they must answer for their lives. Muslims cannot show Allah in pictures or other artwork, since he is beyond human understanding and to try to portray him would be shirk.

Examiner Tip
Although there is only 1 mark per point, you may not be able to answer using a one-word response. You will need to explain in full sentences.

Examiner says
Three good responses are given here.

AO1 Part (d) questions

Some AO1 answers are marked in levels of response. These are the part d) of the questions and are worth 6 marks each. However, just because they are worth 6 marks it does not mean that examiners want to see six short points or develop three points in the answer. Instead the examiner is looking for a level of understanding. The higher the level, then the higher the level of understanding required. This could be done by referring to several points and expanding each a little, or by developing one or two points in greater detail. Below is a sample answer:

> Explain why prayer is important in Islam. **[6 marks]**

Response 1

Prayer is important in Islam because it is one of the duties of a Muslim in the 5 Pillars. It is also important to Muslims because it allows them to get close to God. Finally, there are regular prayer times which allow Muslims to know they are praying with the Ummah.

Examiner says
This is a reasonable Level 2 answer. The candidate has offered three relevant reasons why prayer is important in Islam. However, the reasons have not been developed in greater depth and detail.

Response 2

Regular prayer, or Salah, is important in Islam for a number of reasons. Firstly, it is a requirement of all Muslims to pray five times each day. This is one of the five duties or pillars of Islam. This duty was placed on all Muslims by the Prophet Muhammad (pbuh) and came directly from Allah. Secondly, regular prayer keeps a worshipper closer to Allah. It can allow a believer less chance to do wrong between prayers. This is important because Muslims believe that they will have lived their lives according to Allah's wishes. Finally, regular prayer is important in Islam because the set prayer times bring the whole community together. This creates a sense of belonging amongst Muslims.

Examiner says
This is a much more developed answer. Good explanations are given and a range of key terms are used. This response would achieve a Level 3.

AO2

Part e) of each question in the exam will involve an AO2 question asking you to explain different points of view about a particular issue. It also gives you an opportunity to present your own personal viewpoint. However, please remember that all viewpoints on a particular issue must be backed up with good evidence, argument and reasoning. Part e) of each question is worth 12 marks, or 50 per cent of the total, so it is important to think carefully about how you are going to tackle these questions.

Planning an AO2 answer

These questions want different points of view about a particular issue. Your answer could therefore be structured in the following way:

Paragraph 1: Explain a view that will agree with the statement in the question. Offer evidence, beliefs and teachings to back up the point of view.

Paragraph 2: Explain a different view of what the statement is suggesting. Again you need to offer evidence, beliefs and teachings to back up your point of view.

Paragraph 3: Include your own personal viewpoint about the issue raised. Again you need to offer evidence, belief and arguments to support your point of view. The examiner does not mind which point of view you take, there is no right or wrong answer. Instead the examiner is interested in your ability to reason and argue. If you really do not have a strong point of view on this issue, just simply go for the viewpoint that you can best argue.

Below is an example of an AO2 question and the different levels of response.

> 'Reading the Qur'an is the most important thing in the life of a Muslim.'
>
> **[12 marks]**

Response 1

The Qur'an is important to Muslims. It is a holy book and contains Allah's orders to people. That's why Muslims must read it. Other things are important to Muslims such as doing the Five Pillars.

Examiner says

Two relevant points of view are included here but there is little explanation to back them up. Few key words are used and there is no attempt to reach a conclusion. (Level 1)

Response 2

The Qur'an is important to Muslims because its words came directly from Allah. Anything which comes directly from God has to be very important to Muslims. It contains all the main beliefs which Muslims follow. However, other things are also important to Muslims such as going on pilgrimage, praying five times a day and fasting. I think the Qur'an is important because without it there would not be a Muslim religion.

Response 3

The Qur'an is important to Muslims for several reasons but this does not necessarily mean it is the most important thing in their religious life. It is important to Muslims because it is Allah's direct and final word to the human race. The Qur'an also contains all the beliefs of Islam such as the nature of Allah and warnings about the Day of Judgement. It also forms the basis of Shari'ah Law which guides Muslims in their everyday lives. The Qur'an is therefore significant in the life of a Muslim.

However, other things are also important in the life of a Muslim. It is important that a Muslim acts in the right way in life because they believe in the idea of judgement leading to heaven and hell. Therefore it is also important for a Muslim to pray regularly, give to the poor, fast during Ramadan and perform Hajj at least once in a lifetime. These actions can bring a person closer to Allah than just reading a holy book. I think that the Qur'an is the most important thing in the life of a Muslim.

Response 4

I think the Qur'an is the most important thing in the life of a Muslim. It is the most important thing because it is considered to be Allah's final word to the human race. All modern copies of the Qur'an must be exact copies of the earliest editions. The Qur'an is considered to be the centre of all Muslim belief and practice. It gives clear guidelines about the Day of Judgement and Allah's expectations of people.

Understanding exam language

Examiners try to keep questions short and clear. To do this they use special trigger words to hint at how you should respond to the questions. Below is a list of common trigger words. You should familiarise yourself with these words:

State: Usually used in AO1 questions worth 1–3 marks. This means write down a fact about something, for example: 'State the holy book of Islam.'

Give: This is used instead of 'state' and requires the same sort of response.

Describe: This is used in AO1 questions and means tell the examiner factual information about the item or idea. An example is 'Describe the interior of a mosque', which means write down factual information about what could be found inside a mosque.

Give an account of: This is asking for the same sort of response as **describe**, for example: 'Give an account of the key Muslim beliefs about life after death.'

Explain: This means show that you understand something, for example: 'Explain why Muslims pray five times each day.' An explain response will include some knowledge, but the best responses will give a range of ideas and reasons.

List: This is used instead of 'give' or 'state' and requires the same sort of response.

Why: This word is used as shorthand for explain. Put the word 'explain' in front of it and you will know what to do, for example 'Why do Muslims pray five times each day?' is the same as 'Explain why Muslims pray five times each day'.

How: This can be used to ask you for factual information, for example: 'How do Muslims celebrate the festival of Eid-ul-Adha?' It can also be used for questions that are asking for understanding where there is a mixture of fact and understanding required, for example 'How do Muslims prepare for the Day of Judgement?' means that you can give factual points like following the five pillars or how Muslims live their lives.

Important: This word is used frequently in AO1 part d questions and it indicates that you say why Muslims should or should not do/believe something. An example is 'Explain why the Qur'an is important to Muslims', which means, 'Give reasons to explain why the Qur'an is treated in such a special way in Islam'.

Planning and structuring an answer

In the Grade Studios you have been shown how to build levels of response. This is really important for the AO1 responses to part d) worth 6 marks and the AO2 responses to part e) worth 12 marks. In each case follow this structure:

- Check you really know what the question is asking. In the AO2 questions work out the key word or words in the statement, for example: 'Private worship in Islam is more important than public worship.' The key phrase here is 'more important'. If the answer does not deal with this, then it will be awarded a low mark.

- Make a note of key points to include all AO1 responses and use a diagram to note down viewpoints for AO2.

- Begin your answer with a brief mention of what the question is asking you to do.

- Write clearly and concisely. DON'T WAFFLE.

- Reach a conclusion at the end of your answer. In the case of an AO1 answer this could be a brief linking sentence, for example: 'So we can see why the Hajj is important to Muslims.' In the case of an AO2 answer the conclusion should include a **personal view** (with supporting reasons/argument) and a **brief summing** up of the different views you have expressed.

- Leave a gap of a few lines between each answer. This is in case you wish to add further ideas/information later (if you don't, there is no need to worry).

- If you have any time left at the end of your exam use it constructively. Check your answer makes sense. Check your answer is responding to the question set. Check your use of English, grammar and spelling. Check you have answered the required number of questions. **Remember when you hand in your answer paper at the end of the exam it is probably the last time you will ever see it. Make sure it is your best possible effort.**

Abu Bakr: Muhammad's ﷺ close friend and father-in-law; Sunnis believe he should have succeeded Muhammad ﷺ when he died.

adhan: Call to prayer by the Mu'adhin (one who makes the call to prayer).

al-Fatihah: The name given to the first chapter or Surah of the Qur'an. It follows the form of a prayer.

Ali: Muhammad's ﷺ cousin and son-in-law; Shi'ahs believe he should have succeeded Muhammad ﷺ when he died.

Allah: The Islamic name for God in the Arabic language. Used in preference to the word God, this Arabic term is singular, has no plural, and it is not associated with masculine or feminine characteristics.

aqiqah: A ritual celebration and feast conducted seven days after a birth.

Arafat: A plain, 14 km from Makkah, where pilgrims gather to worship, as part of the Hajj.

Ashura: A major Shi'ah festival which commemorates the martyrdom of Hussein.

calligraphy: A style of decorative writing which is used to illustrate copies of the Qur'an.

du'a: Varying forms of personal prayer and supplication.

Five Pillars of Islam: Five obligatory practices Muslims must follow: Shahadah, Salah, zakah, sawm, Hajj.

Hadith: A collection of sayings of the Prophet Muhammad ﷺ which Muslims consult to help guide them in their understanding.

Hadith of Ali: Shi'ah Muslims have a collection of Hadith from their leader who was Ali, Muhammad's ﷺ cousin.

Hadith of Bukhari: A version of the Hadith compiled by a Muslim scholar named Muhammad ibn Ismail. These are considered to be the most accurate Hadiths attributed to Muhammad ﷺ.

Hadith Qudsi: Hadiths which were spoken by Muhammad ﷺ but came directly from Allah. They are considered the most sacred Hadiths.

Hafiz: A Muslim who is able to memorise the Qur'an by heart. Such individuals are given much honour in a Muslim community.

Hajj: Annual pilgrimage to Makkah, which each Muslim must undertake at least once in their lifetime if he or she has the health and wealth to do so. One of the Five Pillars of Islam.

Hidden Imam: Whether there were five, seven or twelve special Imams, the last mysteriously disappeared and is still believed to be alive, able to guide the current Shi'ah leaders. It is believed that the Hidden Imam will reappear on the Day of Judgement.

Hijrah: Emigration or departure; the term used to describe the prophet Muhammad's ﷺ migration from Makkah to Yathrib (al-Madinah).

Hussein: The grandson of Muhammad ﷺ and Shi'ah leader who died a martyr on the plain of Karbala; Shi'ahs believe he should have been Muhammad's ﷺ successor.

Ibrahim: A prophet of Allah.

ihram: The simple clothing of a pilgrim on Hajj; also the state in which the individual performs Hajj.

imam: A person who leads communal prayer, administers ceremonies and offers their communities spiritual guidance.

Imam: The Imams are twelve individuals who were the direct descendents of Ali. The Imams are regarded as divinely chosen religious figures who act as intermediaries between Allah and the rest of the community. They are considered to be free from sin and infallible.

iqamah: Call to stand up for Salah.

Isa: Jesus; a prophet of Allah.

Isma'il: The son of Ibrahim and Hajar, whom Allah asked Ibrahim to sacrifice, but was then saved by Allah.

jihad: Personal individual struggle against evil in the way of Allah (greater) or collective defence of Muslim community (lesser).

Jumu'ah: The weekly communal Salah, and attendance at the khutbah performed shortly after midday on Fridays.

Ka'bah: Cube-shaped structure in the centre of the grand mosque in Makkah. It was built by Ibrahim and was cleansed of idols by the prophet Muhammad ﷺ. Muslims pray in the direction of this building.

Karbala: The place in modern Iraq where the Shi'ah leader Hussein was martyred. A major centre of Shi'ah pilgrimage today.

khalifah: Steward or custodian (of the earth).

khutbah: Talk delivered on special occasions such as the Jumu'ah and Id prayers.

mahr: A gift – usually money paid by the husband to the wife.

Makkah: The city where the prophet Muhammad ﷺ was born.

martyr: A person who dies for a belief or cause.

mihrab: Niche or alcove in a Mosque wall, indicating the qiblah – the direction of Makkah, towards which all Muslims face to perform Salah. It helps the worshipper to remain focused.

Mina: A place near Makkah where pilgrims stay during 10–12 Dhul-Hijjah and perform some of the activities of the Hajj.

minaret: Tall spires with onion-shaped crowns, usually either free standing or much taller than any surrounding support structure.

inbar: Rostrum; platform; dais. The stand from which the imam delivers the khutbah or speech in the mosque or praying ground.

onogamy: Having only one partner at a time.

osque: Muslim place of worship (prostration).

Muáwiya: The fifth khalifah, cousin of the murdered Uthman, and father of Yazid.

Muhammad ﷺ: The name of the final prophet.

Night of Power: The night when the first part of the Qur'an was revealed to the Prophet Muhammad ﷺ.

nikah: Traditional marriage ritual – the wedding.

polygamy: A legal marriage of a man to more than one woman.

prophets: Messengers of Allah.

qiblah: Direction which Muslims face when performing Salah – towards the Ka'bah.

Qur'an: Allah's word revealed through Muhammad ﷺ to humanity; the most important holy book of Islam.

Ramadan: The ninth month of the Islamic calendar during which fasting is required from just before dawn until sunset as ordered by Allah in the Qur'an.

sa'y: The practice of walking or hastening between the hills Safa and Marwah as part of the Hajj, symbolising Hajar's search for water.

sadaqah: Voluntary payment or action for charitable purposes.

Safa and Marwah: Two hills in Makkah between which Hajar ran to search for water for Isma'il. Walking or running between these hills is part of the Hajj.

Sahih al-Bukhari: A collection of Hadith made by Muhammad ibn Ismail. He was born in Bukhara. These are believed to be the most genuine Hadith.

sajjadah: A prayer mat which is a small and portable carpet that Muslims put on the floor when they perform their prayers.

Salah: Obligatory set prayer five times a day; one of the Five Pillars of Islam.

sawm: Fasting in the month of Ramadan; one of the Five Pillars of Islam.

Shahadah: Declaration of faith; one of the Five Pillars of Islam.

Shi'ah: A Muslim who believes Ali should have succeeded Muhammad ﷺ, because he was Muhammad's ﷺ cousin. They form about 11 per cent of the total Muslim population.

shirk: Associating anything with God; the most serious sin that a Muslim can commit.

subhah: String of beads used to count recitations in worship.

Sufi: A group within Islam, concerned with mystical experience and with developing their relationship with Allah. Sufis can be Sunni or Shi'ah.

Sunnah: Model practices, customs and traditions of Muhammad ﷺ.

Sunni: A Muslim who believes Abu Bakr should have succeeded Muhammad ﷺ. They follow the Sunnah or the way of Muhammad ﷺ. Sunni Muslims form about 89 per cent of the Muslim population worldwide.

Surah: A chapter in the Qur'an. There are 114 of these arranged from longest to shortest.

tawaf: Circling the Ka'bah seven times in an anti-clockwise direction in worship of Allah, performed as part of the Hajj.

tawhid: Belief in the Oneness of Allah.

ummah: Worldwide community of Muslims; the nation of Islam.

Uthman: The khalifah or successor to Muhammad ﷺ who organised the official version of the Qur'an.

walimah: The feast which follows a wedding.

wudu: Ritual washing before praying.

Yazid: The opponent of Hussein at Karbala, and son of Muáwiya.

zakah: Purification of wealth by payment of annual welfare due; one of the Five Pillars of Islam.